PROPHET ARISE

JOHN ECKHARDT

CHARISMA
HOUSE

P9-DTB-887

Most CHARISMA HOUSE BOOK GROUP products are available at special quantity discounts for bulk purchase for sales promotions, premiums, fund-raising, and educational needs. For details, write Charisma House Book Group, 600 Rinehart Road, Lake Mary, Florida 32746, or telephone (407) 333-0600.

PROPHET, ARISE! by John Eckhardt
Published by Charisma House
Charisma Media/Charisma House Book Group
600 Rinehart Road
Lake Mary, Florida 32746
www.charismahouse.com

Unless otherwise noted, all Scripture quotations are taken from the Holy Bible, Modern English Version. Copyright © 2014 by Military Bible Association. Used by permission. All rights reserved.

Scripture quotations marked AMP are from the Amplified Bible. Copyright © 1954, 1958, 1962, 1964, 1965, 1987 by The Lockman Foundation. Used by permission.

Scripture quotations marked CJB are from The Complete Jewish Bible. Copyright © 1998 by David H. Stern. All rights reserved.

Scripture quotations marked EXB are from *The Expanded Bible*. Copyright © 2011 by Thomas Nelson, Inc. Used by permission. All rights reserved.

Scripture quotations marked GNT are from the Good News Translation (Today's English Version, Second Edition). Copyright © 1992 American Bible Society. All rights reserved.

Cover design by Justin Evans

Visit the author's website at www.johneckhardtministries.com.

Library of Congress Cataloging-in-Publication Data:
Eckhardt, John, 1957-
  Prophet, arise! / by John Eckhardt. -- First edition.
      pages cm
  Includes bibliographical references.
  ISBN 978-1-62998-638-8 (trade paper) -- ISBN 978-1-62998-
639-5 (e-book)
  1. Prophecy--Christianity. 2. Gifts, Spiritual. I. Title.
  BR115.P8E36 2015
  234'.13--dc23

                                    2014048670

Parts of this book were previously published as *Prayers That Rout Demons*, ISBN: 978-1-59979-246-0, copyright © 2008, *God's Covenant With You for Your Family*, ISBN: 978-1-62136-012-4, copyright © 2013, and *God Still Speaks*, ISBN: 978-1-59979-475-4, copyright © 2009.

While the author has made every effort to provide accurate Internet addresses at the time of publication, neither the publisher nor the author assumes any responsibility for errors or for changes that occur after publication.

16 17 18 19 20 — 11 10 9 8 7
Printed in the United States of America

CONTENTS

ARISE AND SHINE

Arise, shine, for your light has come, and the glory of the LORD
*has risen upon you. For darkness shall cover the earth and
deep darkness the peoples; but the* LORD *shall rise upon you,
and His glory shall be seen upon you. The nations shall come
to your light and kings to the brightness of your rising.*

—ISAIAH 60:1–3

I T IS TIME for the prophets to arise and shine. Your light has come. God stirs His prophets whenever there is darkness. Those in darkness need to see the light. Those in darkness need to hear the voice of the Lord. There is a new glory coming on the prophets. There is a new honor and favor coming upon them. Those who have been ignored and oppressed are now coming forth. Those who have been in despair are now being encouraged. There is a global community of prophets that is being challenged and called. They are in every nation and city. They will not be hidden anymore. The nations will see you. Your cities will hear you. The churches will acknowledge you.

This book is a call to the prophets. It is a word to the prophets. It is a call to arise. It is a call to shine. Many prophets have been in the dark. They have not known their true calling. Religion and tradition have hindered them. But now they will see. Now they will come out of the dark. They will come out of the caves.

> David departed from there and escaped to the cave of Adullam. And when his brothers and all his father's house heard it, they went down to him there.
>
> —1 SAMUEL 22:1

David fled to the cave. Many prophets have fled to the cave.

When Jezebel killed the prophets of the LORD, Obadiah took
a hundred prophets and hid them in groups of fifty in a cave
and fed them with bread and water.

—1 KINGS 18:4

God has sustained you in the cave. God has fed you bread and
water. God would not let you die. It is time to come out of your caves.
It is time to come out of the shadows. It is time to prophesy. It is time
to fulfill your call.

It is also a time of restoration. It is a time for healing and deliverance. Prophets will be healed and made whole. Prophets who have
been hurt, discouraged, frustrated, cast out, mistreated, and persecuted are being touched by heaven.

> For I will restore health to you, and I will heal you of your
> wounds, says the LORD, because they called you an outcast,
> saying, "This is Zion whom no man cares for."
>
> —JEREMIAH 30:17

Men will once again seek after you. They will say, "What is the
word of the Lord?" You will no longer be an outcast.

Let any harvest the enemy has stolen be restored.

> And I will compensate you for the years the locusts have
> eaten—the larval locust, the hopper locust, and the fledging
> locust—My great army which I sent against you.
>
> —JOEL 2:25

With the truths from this book, you will be better able to identify
who you are. You will learn why you are different and why you are
configured the way you are. You have been designed by God for His
plans and purposes. You have been created for God's glory.

> Even everyone who is called by My name, for I have created
> him for My glory; I have formed him, and I have made him.
>
> —ISAIAH 43:7

Fresh oil is coming to the prophets from heaven. God is pouring it out upon His prophets. God has seen you, and your cup will overflow. God is the God of the overflow.

> But my horn You have exalted like the horn of the wild ox;
> You have anointed me with fresh oil.
>
> —Psalm 92:10

There is a fresh anointing coming on the prophets. You may have been anointed once before, but get ready for something new. David was anointed three times. Each anointing took him to another level of power and authority.

Get ready, prophets, for new levels of power and authority. Get ready for a new flow of prophecy. Your utterances will get stronger and deeper. You ear will become more sensitive to the voice of God.

> You shall arise, and have mercy upon Zion, for the time to favor her, indeed, the appointed time has come.
>
> —Psalm 102:13

This is the set time of favor. This is the set time to arise and shine. This is a new season for the prophets. The winter is over. Your spring season has arrived.

> The flowers appear on the earth; the time of the singing has come, and the voice of the turtledove is heard in our land.
>
> —Song of Songs 2:12

God loves His prophets. He has seen their condition. He speaks now to arise and shine. Your light has come, and the glory of the Lord is risen upon thee.

WHY WE NEED YOU

The tendency of men and movements to get off track in a short period of time is confirmed in the Bible and in the history of the church. The prophet is the one who warns and calls men and movements to get back on track.

1. Men and movements can begin in the Spirit and quickly end up in the flesh.

2. Men and movements can get away from the mandate to advance the kingdom and instead begin to build empires.

3. Men and movements can become controlling and exclusive.

4. Greed and mammon can begin to manifest in men and movements.

5. The standards of righteousness and holiness can begin to fall in a short period of time.

6. Pride and vanity can begin to replace humility and meekness.

7. Error and false teaching can creep into men and movements quickly.

8. The traditions of men can be elevated to the position of Scripture.

9. Ungodly people can rise to leadership positions through manipulation and seduction.

10. Men and movements can stagnate and cease to progress.

11. Men and movements can become obsolete and irrelevant to the present generation in a short period of time.

12. Men and movements can cease to be the salt of the earth.

13. Men and movements can become carnal and worldly and begin to compromise.

14. Men and movements can lose their fire and zeal, and rest on past accomplishments.

When there are no prophets

Prophets, along with other ministry gifts, are a sign of God is presence in the church (Ps. 68:18). Whenever God's presence departed from Israel in Old Testament times, one mark of His forsaking them was that there was no longer any prophet among them (Ps. 74:1, 9).

> You have ascended on high, You have led captivity captive;
> You have received gifts from people, yes, even from the rebellious, that the LORD God might dwell among them.
> —PSALM 68:18

> We do not see our signs; there is no longer any prophet, nor is there among us any who knows how long.
> —PSALM 74:9

There were no prophets in Israel when Samuel was born. The priesthood was corrupt, and the nation was in apostasy. Samuel brought a new level of blessing to Israel and transitioned Israel to one of its greatest periods of power and glory.

> Now the boy Samuel was ministering to the LORD before Eli. And the word of the LORD was rare in those days. There was no vision coming forth.
> —1 SAMUEL 3:1

When there are no prophets, there is a famine. Let the famine be broken over cities and regions where there is no prophetic release.

> The time is coming, says the Lord GOD, when I will send a famine on the land, not a famine of bread, nor a thirst for water, but of hearing the words of the LORD. They will wander from sea to sea, and from north to east; they will run back and forth to seek the word of the LORD, but they will not find it.
> —AMOS 8:11–12

How This Book Was Birthed

At the end of November and the beginning of December 2014 the Lord began to stir my heart to release His word of encouragement and confirmation to the many prophets who have been silenced and shut down in their local churches. So during this time on my Facebook page I began posting statuses on prophets day after day. What I began writing was not planned. It was not something written down ahead of time. It just began to flow from my heart. As a result, I have received thousands of likes and comments from people around the world saying how they have been touched. Some have received healing and release as they read the statuses. The Lord told me to keep pouring out the oil as long as there were vessels receiving, so I will continue until it stops.

> So she left him and shut the door behind her and her sons, and they kept bringing vessels to her, and she kept pouring. When the vessels were full, she said to her son, "Bring me another vessel." But he said to her, "There is not another vessel." And the oil ceased.
>
> —2 Kings 4:5–6

This book is a compilation of what started on Facebook. People commented on being so blessed that they wanted all the posts in book form. This is the reason for this book. It has been edited and organized to fit this new method of delivery, but it is all still *rhema* for the prophet. If you want to see what God continued to reveal to me even as this book went to press, go to Facebook and search the hashtag *#prophets*. You can also get a full scope of the office of a prophet in my book *God Still Speaks*.

I realize that the posts from which this book is derived are primarily about prophets, but many of these truths apply to apostles and other ministry gifts as well. The Lord led me to zero in on prophets because they have often been misunderstood and sometimes have not understood themselves. The truth is, we need all the gifts, but we desperately need prophets to be awakened and released.

Let me also add that although everyone is not a prophet, we can all be prophetic. That is why this book is good for all God's people. God desires that we all be "prophets" in the sense that we all should hear God and be obedient in releasing His word. The characteristics of prophets should, to some degree, be the characteristics of all Spirit-filled believers. Joel prophesied that God would pour His spirit out on *all* flesh—sons, daughters, young men, and old men.

One of my life scriptures is Numbers 11:29, "Moses said to him, 'Are you jealous for my sake? Oh, that all the people of the LORD were prophets, and that the LORD would put His Spirit upon them!'" Moses's desire was prophesied by Joel and fulfilled on the Day of Pentecost with the outpouring of the Holy Spirit. In this sense we are all prophets or prophetic to some degree. So encouragement, mentorship, and activation of prophets is needed for those beyond the select group of the so-called elite prophets. You will find the truths in this book appropriate to your life regardless of your specific calling. Apostles, prophets, evangelists, pastors, teachers, and *all* believers should be prophetic and have the heart of the greatest prophet, Jesus Christ, the Son of God.

I pray that you are blessed and strengthened by what you read. I pray that you will know that you are not forgotten by God. He has not sidelined you. You are not crazy. Prophet, arise! Come out of your cave and be encouraged to speak forth the word of the Lord.

PROPHET, ARISE

by John Eckhardt

The Lord is setting a flame
To His prophets around the globe,
They are coming forth with power,
It is time to arise.

They are coming out of the cave.
It is a new day of boldness,
So now come forth,
It is time to arise.

You will no longer hide,
You will now speak forth.
God has seen your tears,
It is time to arise.

He has heard your prayers,
You have not been forgotten,
The day of hiding is over,
It is time to arise.

You now know who you are,
No more confusion,
I have called you by name
It is time to arise.

You are special to Me,
A new breed set apart,
I do not reject you,
It is time to arise.

Hear me when I call you,
And now obey My voice,
Your God is now speaking,
It is time to arise.

1

THE MAKING OF A PROPHET

He will sit as a refiner and purifier of silver;
he will purify the sons of Levi, and refine them like gold and silver,
and they will present to the LORD offerings in righteousness.

—MALACHI 3:3

OD PUTS A prophet through a process of refinement. God purges the prophet and develops their character. The prophet has to respond to the dealings of God in their own life before they can effectively deal with the problems in the lives of others. Sometimes as a prophet you will feel as if you are in a furnace. You may find yourself saying, "God, why are You dealing so strongly with me? Why don't You deal with everyone else like this?" Don't give up, prophet. Go through the process.

> The fining pot is for silver and the furnace for gold, but the LORD tries the hearts.
>
> —PROVERBS 17:3

LET GOD PURGE YOU

A prophet is a vessel. God purges His vessels. God will take the dross (impurities) out of your life. You have to become the raw material to be a prophetic vessel. Go through the process. Let the fire burn.

> Take away the dross from the silver, and there will come forth a vessel for the finer.
>
> —PROVERBS 25:4

> Take away the dross from the silver, and the smith has material for a vessel.
>
> —PROVERBS 25:4, ESV

Prophet, don't allow guilt, shame, and condemnation prevent you from accepting and walking in your calling. Many prophets struggle with feelings of inadequacy as a result of their past. Isaiah was purged and sent. Allow the Lord to purge you from sins of the past, walk clean before the Lord, and fulfill your call.

> And I said: "Woe is me! For I am undone because I am a man of unclean lips, and I dwell in the midst of a people of unclean lips. For my eyes have seen the King, the LORD of Hosts."
>
> —ISAIAH 6:5

Prophets must be faithful.

Moses distinguished himself as a prophet by his faithfulness. Be faithful to the call and commission.

> And he said, And my servant Moses is not such, the which is most faithful in all mine house; (Then he said, But my servant Moses is not such a prophet, for he alone is most faithful in all my household;)
>
> —NUMBERS 12:7, WYC

> My eyes shall be favorable to the faithful in the land, that they may live with me; he who walks in a blameless manner, he shall serve me
>
> —PSALM 101:6

GOD CHOOSES PROPHETS BY HIS GRACE

> But by the grace of God I am what I am. And His grace toward me was not in vain. I labored more abundantly than all of them, yet not I, but the grace of God which was with me.
>
> —1 CORINTHIANS 15:10

Prophets understand grace. They know God's strength is by grace. They understand that they cannot do this in their own strength. Prophets depend on the grace of God (His strength, favor, power, and ability). They understand that without God they can do nothing.

Prophets will find themselves in situations when they have to depend on grace.

> I can do nothing of Myself. As I hear, I judge. My judgment is just, because I seek not My own will, but the will of the Father who sent Me.
>
> —JOHN 5:30

Prophets are God's choice, not man's.

God calls all kinds of people to be prophets. The Lord chose the foolish things to confound the things that are wise (1 Cor. 1:27–29). David was an obscure shepherd boy. Amos was not a prophet or a prophet's son. God calls people who would not qualify by the standards of men. Prophets are not determined by men, but by God. God's choice is a challenge and rebuke against the pride of men.

God even calls the rebellious. (See more on this in chapter 6.)

> You have ascended on high, You have led captivity captive; You have received gifts from people, yes, even from the rebellious, that the LORD God might dwell among them.
>
> —PSALM 68:18

Prophets are taught by God.

There are things that you can learn directly from God. This is what happens to prophets. Prophets know things that are not taught by men. Jesus knew more than all the religious leaders of His day. They marveled at His knowledge. Jesus had not attended their schools.

> The people were amazed [marveled] and said, "This man has never studied in school. How did he learn so much?"
>
> —JOHN 7:15, EXB

THE PROPHET'S ANOINTING

The prophet's words are anointed and carry power. When prophets speak, things happen. When prophets speak, things change. When prophets speak, God moves. The word of a prophet is like a fire that burns and a hammer that breaks the rock in pieces.

Open your mouth, prophet, and speak. God will back you up. He will confirm the words of His servants.

> Is not My word like fire, says the LORD, and like a hammer that breaks the rock in pieces?
>
> —JEREMIAH 23:29

> Who confirms the word of His servant, and performs the counsel of His messengers.
>
> —ISAIAH 44:26

God commands His prophets to prophesy. When they do, there is a noise, a shaking, a coming together. Dead things come to life. Dry bones live again. The prophets' words bring life. They release breath.

> So I prophesied as I was commanded. And as I prophesied, there was a noise and shaking. And the bones came together, bone to its bone....So I prophesied as He commanded me, and the breath came into them, and they lived and stood up upon their feet, an exceeding great army.
>
> —EZEKIEL 37:7, 10

Prophets have to prophesy when God is speaking. When God is speaking, who can keep from prophesying? His prophets can't help but prophesy. Who will not prophesy? What prophet can keep quiet? Who can refuse to prophesy? Who can do anything but prophesy? Some may want the prophets to be quiet, but they can't help but prophesy.

> The lion has roared; who will not fear? The Lord GOD has spoken; who can but prophesy?
>
> —AMOS 3:8

The word of the Lord will come to prophets, even when people try to lock them up. Shut down...

> Now the word of the LORD came unto Jeremiah while he was shut up in the court of the prison.
>
> —JEREMIAH 39:15

Prophets have to have a way to vent and release what God gives them, otherwise they feel like they will burst.

> See, my belly is like wine that has no vent; it is ready to burst like new wineskins.
>
> —Job 32:19

This release can happen in the form of weeping, speaking, writing, singing, dancing, or praying.

Prophets are not to be told what to see and say.

You cannot make prophets do what you want them to do. They are not to be used for your benefit and desire, but they are created for God's purposes. You are in trouble when you try to make them see and say what you want them to see and say. Prophets are independent spokesmen.

> They say to the seers, "See no more visions!" and to the prophets, "Give us no more visions of what is right! Tell us pleasant things, prophesy illusions."
>
> —Isaiah 30:10, niv

Israel wanted the seers and prophets to see and say what they wanted to hear. Prophets can only see and say what the Lord desires.

The sweet and the bitter

Many people want to hear sweet messages, but not bitter. That which is bitter is unpleasant to the taste. Prophets are not sent only to speak that which is pleasant and sweet. Prophets will also have to speak the bitter (sour).

> So I went to the angel and said to him, "Give me the little scroll." He said to me, "Take it and eat it. 'It will turn your stomach sour, but in your mouth it will be as sweet as honey.'"
>
> —Revelation 10:9

Prophets don't preach what is popular, neither do they preach to be popular. They often preach a truth that makes them unpopular.

The prophet…is unpopular because he opposes the popular in morality and spirituality. In a day of faceless politicians and voiceless preachers, there is not a more urgent national need than that we cry to God for a prophet![1]

—LEONARD RAVENHILL

Don't mock the messengers of God.

But they continued to jest regarding the messengers of God, despising His word and making fun of His prophets until the wrath of the LORD came up against His people, until there was no remedy.

—2 CHRONICLES 36:16

Prophets are not hirelings (Balaam).

Prophets cannot be bought. They are not for sale. Balaam was for hire. Balaam died a soothsayer. You don't rent a prophet.

The children of Israel killed Balaam son of Beor, who practiced divination, with the sword along with the rest of the slain.

—JOSHUA 13:22

Peter said to him, "May your money perish with you, because you thought you could purchase the gift of God with money!"

—ACTS 8:20

The error of Balaam

Balaam is a man who had visions, the knowledge of God, and heard the word of God, yet he died a soothsayer. His problem was the love of money. Prophets can become fakes if they do not guard their hearts from the god of mammon. Balaam later died at the hands of Israel as they possessed Canaan (Josh. 13:22).

He hath said, which heard the words of God, and knew the knowledge of the most High, which saw the vision of the Almighty, falling into a trance, but having his eyes open.

—NUMBERS 24:16, KJV

They have forsaken the right way and have gone astray. They follow the way of Balaam the son of Beor, who loved the wages of wickedness.

—2 Peter 2:15

Balaam represents the merchandising prophet. It seems that he had genuine prophetic gifts at some point, but that he was caught by the trap of greed. He became a "prophet for hire." The book of Jude deals with false prophets/teachers and says that they "have run greedily in the error of Balaam for profit" (Jude 1:11).[2]

—Jake Kail

Prophets are not owned by people and organizations; they are owned only by God. The prophet is devoted to God and truth, not institutions, organizations, religions, doctrines, and creeds!

The prophet's mouth

Prophets will say things others will not say. God touches the prophet's mouth. When God touches a person's mouth, He puts power and authority in their words. Prophets pray, sing, preach, teach, and prophesy. Their mouths are anointed. Their words are anointed. Their prayers are anointed. Their songs are anointed.

Then the Lord put forth his hand and touched my mouth. And the Lord said to me, "Now, I have put My words in your mouth."

—Jeremiah 1:9

The prophetic word will not return void.

It will not return unfulfilled. God sends His word for a purpose. The prophetic word has an assignment.

So shall My word be that goes forth from My mouth; it shall not return to Me void, but it shall accomplish that which I please, and it shall prosper in the thing for which I sent it.

—Isaiah 55:11

The prophet's seal

A seal is a mark. It represents something that is genuine. Those who cry and weep for sin and rebellion are marked by God. God knows His prophets. God places His mark on them. A mark represents ownership. God marks His people and seals them.

> And the LORD said to him, "Go through the midst of the city, through the midst of Jerusalem, and set a mark upon the foreheads of the men who sigh and groan for all the abominations that are done in its midst."
>
> —EZEKIEL 9:4

The prophet's mantle

The mantle was the cloak that was worn by prophets. The cloak represented the power and authority of the prophet. Elisha caught Elijah's mantle, then used it to separate the Jordan River. This shows the power of what a prophet carries. Prophets have power and authority from heaven. This power and authority is real.

> And he took the robe of Elijah that fell from him, and struck the water, and said, "Where is the LORD, God of Elijah?" When he had struck the water, it parted from one side to the other, and Elisha crossed over.
>
> —2 KINGS 2:14

YOU MUST OVERCOME FEAR

The Lord will put you in situations where you must overcome fear. You will have to learn to overcome criticism, rejection, jealous people, and the like. This is part of the making of a prophet. The Lord is building courage in you. You will have to make decisions that some people won't agree with. You will have to take a stand. You cannot please everyone. You may lose some relationships over this one.

Prophets must overcome the fear of man.

This can be a major battle for prophets. The fear of man brings a snare. You cannot fear man, the call, criticism, rejection, persecution, or intimidation and be strong in the prophetic. Fear will short-circuit your prophetic flow. Everyone has to overcome some kind of fear. You are not alone. God will deliver you from all your fears and give you the courage you need.

> "Do not be afraid of their faces. For I am with you to deliver you," says the LORD.
>
> —JEREMIAH 1:8

> Do not fear those who kill the body but are not able to kill the soul. But rather fear Him who is able to destroy both soul and body in hell.
>
> —MATTHEW 10:28

> The fear of man brings a snare, but whoever puts his trust in the LORD will be safe.
>
> —PROVERBS 29:25

Prophets are not men-pleasing.

> For am I now seeking the approval of men or of God? Or am I trying to please men? For if I were still trying to please men, I would not be the servant of Christ.
>
> —GALATIANS 1:10

The prophet's desire is to please God, not men. You cannot be a servant of Christ and please men. Prophets don't seek the approval of men. The prophet's priority is to please God. Inordinate people pleasing brings you into bondage by enslaving you to everyone whom you desire to please.

Prophets must obey God rather than man.

> Peter and the other apostles answered, "We must obey God rather than men."
>
> —ACTS 5:29

Although this is spoken by an apostle (and it applies to apostles as well), this describes a prophet perfectly. When confronted with a choice, the prophet will obey God. Man cannot be above God to the prophet. God's commands trump all.

Prophets don't live off of the praise of men.

> Men love the acknowledgments of men, particularly prestigious men, but we have got to be weaned away from that necessity. It is a process; it does not take place in a day. Every time that God brings us to that place of weaning, we have got to submit to it, until we come to the place where we do not need it. We need to come to the place where we are not only indifferent to the applause of men, but also to their criticisms and reproaches.[3]
>
> —ART KATZ

> For they loved the praise of men more than the praise of God.
> —JOHN 12:43

> But he is a Jew who is one inwardly. And circumcision is of the heart, by the Spirit, and not by the letter. His praise is not from men, but from God.
> —ROMANS 2:29

Prophets don't live by man's honor; prophets look for honor from God.

Jesus did not look for or receive honor from men. Jesus received honor from the Father. Prophets have always had to live without honor from men. God does not want you to depend on man's honor. The Father's honor is the most important thing to prophets.

> Jesus said to them, "A prophet is not without honor, except in his own country, and among his own relatives, and in his own house."
> —MARK 6:4

> I do not receive honor from men.
> —JOHN 5:41

> Jesus answered, "If I glorify Myself, My glory is nothing. It
> is My Father who glorifies Me, of whom you say that He is
> your God."
>
> —JOHN 8:54

Prophets, you must be willing to stand alone if you have to.

Fear will cause men to run and hide. Just ask Jesus and Paul.

> "But all this was done that the Scriptures of the prophets might
> be fulfilled." Then all the disciples forsook Him and fled.
>
> —MATTHEW 26:56

> At my first defense no one stood with me, but everyone for-
> sook me. May it not be charged against them.
>
> —2 TIMOTHY 4:16

Prophets can be excommunicated for the truth.

The fear of excommunication—of being put out of the synagogue,
of being put out of the church or denomination—has always been
a way that religious systems control men. The Pharisees threatened
anyone who confessed Christ with excommunication. Are you willing
to be excommunicated because of the truth?

The early church leaders were excommunicated. Martin Luther
and John Hus were excommunicated. The reformers were excommunicated.

Excommunication is really a kind of banishment, a punishment
that's handed out by a church when one of its members breaks some
important church rule. The Latin root is *excommunicare*, meaning
"put out of the community," which is just what happens when a person
is excommunicated.

> His parents said this, because they feared the Jews. For the
> Jews had already agreed that if anyone confessed that He was
> the Christ, he would be put out of the synagogue.
>
> —JOHN 9:22

> They will put you out of the synagogues. Yes, the time is
> coming that whoever kills you will think that he is offering
> a service to God.
>
> —John 16:2

Fear of confrontation is the enemy of a prophet.

> Go to Pharaoh in the morning as he goes out to the river.
> Confront him on the bank of the Nile, and take in your hand
> the staff that was changed into a snake.
>
> —Exodus 7:15, niv

> Son of man, confront Jerusalem with her detestable practices.
>
> —Ezekiel 16:2, niv

Prophets are sometimes accused of being crazy and having a devil.

Jesus was called a Samaritan and accused of having a devil.
Prophets are often called "rebellious," "religious," "deep," "spooky,"
and "crazy," especially by religious systems that are confronted with
the truth.

> The Jews there answered, "We say you are a Samaritan. We
> say a demon is making you crazy! Are we not right when we
> say this?"
>
> —John 8:48, erv

> Then the Jews said to Him, "Now we know that You have a
> demon. Abraham and the prophets died, and You say, 'If a
> man keeps My word, he shall never taste death.'"
>
> —John 8:52

"Judge not" is the biblical phrase used to shut the mouths of prophets.

Jesus was referring to a critical, condemning, fault-finding, nit-
picking, and self-righteous spirit (outer judgment). The biblical refer-
ence to "judge not" does not mean that wickedness and evil should not
be exposed and rebuked. Jesus is referring to unrighteous judgment,

and not to righteous judgment. Jesus exposed and rebuked the Phari-sees for their wickedness.

> Do not judge and criticize and condemn others, so that you may not be judged and criticized and condemned yourselves.
>
> —MATTHEW 7:1, AMP

> Do not judge according to appearance, but practice righteous judgment.
>
> —JOHN 7:24

HOW TO HANDLE HARDSHIP AND OPPOSITION

Demons hate prophets. Witches and warlocks hate prophets. Jezebel hates prophets. Prophets are a threat to the works of darkness. Prophets expose the works of the enemy. Prophets are on the enemy's hit list. God protects His prophets. God sustains them. Don't be afraid of the enemy. No weapon formed against you will prosper.

> No weapon that is formed against you shall prosper, and every tongue that shall rise against you in judgment, you shall condemn. This is the heritage of the servants of the LORD, and their vindication is from Me, says the LORD.
>
> —ISAIAH 54:17

> When Jezebel killed the prophets of the LORD, Obadiah took a hundred prophets and hid them in groups of fifty in a cave and fed them with bread and water..
>
> —1 KINGS 18:4

God sustains prophets. They don't have to depend on men and religious systems to survive. Prophets depend on God. They must be free to speak for the Lord. True prophets don't eat at Jezebel's table.

> Arise, go to Zarephath, which belongs to Sidon, and live there. I have commanded a widow there to provide for you.
>
> —1 KINGS 17:9

Now send word out and gather for me all Israel on Mount
Carmel, along with the four hundred and fifty prophets of
Baal and the four hundred prophets of Asherah who eat at
Jezebel's table.

—1 KINGS 18:19

Elijah was fed by ravens. God was his source and provider.
Prophets depend on God for sustenance. Prophets need God's sustenance because they are often rejected by men. Prophet, expect to
receive miraculous provision from God.

"Go from here and turn eastward and hide by the Kerith brook,
which is east of the Jordan. You shall drink from the brook,
and I have commanded the ravens to feed you there." So he
went and did according to the word of the LORD, for he went
and lived by the Kerith brook, which is east of the Jordan.

—1 KINGS 17:3–5

God preserves His prophets. Don't be fooled; you cannot kill
them all.

Were you not told what I did when Jezebel killed the prophets
of the LORD, how I hid a hundred men of the LORD's prophets
in groups of fifty in a cave and fed them with bread and water?

—1 KINGS 18:13

God hates when His prophets are mistreated. Prophets can be mistreated, persecuted, ignored, called crazy, rejected, overlooked, isolated,
muzzled, and passed over. Prophets are often persecuted by the systems they cry out against. This is nothing new. God vindicates His
prophets, defends them, and deals with the systems that mistreat them.

Saying, "Do not touch my anointed ones, and do no harm to
my prophets."

—PSALM 105:15

Now Jeremiah was still coming in and going out among the people, for they had not yet put him into prison.

—JEREMIAH 37:4

Get tough.

If you are a prophet, you will have to develop some toughness. Be prepared to put on the camel's hair and eat locusts and wild honey.

This same John had clothing made of camel's hair, a leather belt around his waist, and his food was locusts and wild honey.

—MATTHEW 3:4

You must be tough, strong enough to withstand adverse conditions or rough or careless handling.

Shake off the dust.

Prophets have to learn how to "shake off the dust." Prophets want everyone to receive the truth and be blessed, but sometimes it just does not happen that way. You can't make people do what the Lord says. Sometimes you have to leave and "shake off the dust."

Whoever will not receive you, nor hear your words, when you depart out of that house or city, shake off the dust of your feet

—MATTHEW 10:14

Be careful.

If you are rejected, don't pick up demons of hurt and rejection. Don't let those demons in your life. Remember the word of the Lord to Samuel:

The Lord said to Samuel, "...For it is not you they have rejected, but Me they have rejected from reigning over them.

—1 SAMUEL 8:7

It's not about you; it's about the Lord. Rejoice, and be exceedingly glad.

Blessed are you when men revile you, and persecute you, and say all kinds of evil against you falsely for My sake. Rejoice and be very glad, because great is your reward in heaven, for in this manner they persecuted the prophets who were before you.

—MATTHEW 5:11–12

Rejoice, prophets!

Prophets know what it is to weep. Prophets know what it is to grieve. Prophets also need to rejoice. Prophets must learn to rejoice even when things don't look good. Learn from the prophet Habakkuk. "Weeping may endure for a night…"

Though the fig tree does not blossom, nor fruit be on the vines; though the yield of the olive fails, and the fields produce no food; though the flocks are cut off from the fold, and there be no herd in the stalls—yet I will rejoice in the Lord; I will exult in the God of my salvation. The Lord God is my strength; He will make my feet like hinds' feet, and He will make me walk on my high places. To the Music Director: with my stringed instruments.

—HABAKKUK 3:17–19

For His anger endures but a moment, in His favor is life; weeping may endure for a night, but joy comes in the morning.

—PSALM 30:5

Prophets sometimes feel they are crying in the wilderness.

John was a prophet crying in the wilderness. He was in the deserts. The desert represents isolation and separation. The people came to the wilderness to hear him. Don't despair, prophet. Those who want to hear will hear.

For this is he who was spoken of by the prophet Isaiah, saying: "The voice of one crying in the wilderness: 'Prepare the way of the Lord; make His paths straight.' "…Then Jerusalem, and all Judea, and all the region around the Jordan went out to him.

—MATTHEW 3:3, 5

Roll your works upon the Lord.

Roll your works upon the Lord [commit and trust them wholly to Him; He will cause your thoughts to become agreeable to His will, and] so shall your plans be established and succeed.

—PROVERBS 16:3, AMP

A man's heart devises his way, but the LORD directs his steps.

—PROVERBS 16:9

GENERAL FUNCTIONS OF A PROPHET

See, I have this day set you over the nations and over the kingdoms, to root out and to pull down, to destroy and to throw down, to build and to plant.

—JEREMIAH 1:10

Prophets pull down that which God did not build! Prophets root up that which God did not plant! Prophets destroy what God wants destroyed!

Prophets release ministries.

God uses prophets to send out ministries. Prophets enjoy releasing and seeing ministers released. Prophets love to see people activated and released into their God-given destinies. They love to see the plans and purposes of God come to pass in peoples' lives.

The plans and purposes of God are their passion.

Prophets don't like being in ministries where no one is released. Prophets don't like seeing the wrong people released.

It is the ministry of prophets to pray over and lay hands on those being separated unto special ministry (Acts 13:2). The prophets and teachers at Antioch heard the Spirit say separate Paul and Barnabas.

They separated them, laid hands on them, and sent them out. Prophets help us release ministries.

Prophets do more than prophesy

They also pray, intercede, discern, weep, worship, sing, declare, announce, pronounce, renounce, decree, build, break, uproot, warn, correct, renew, revive, restore, reform, counsel, help, assist, strengthen, see, expose, preach, teach, disciple, train, release, equip, impart, activate, stir up, break down, tear down, plant, water, send, guard, protect, watch, prepare, open, close, gather, sound the alarm, blow the trumpet, stand in the gap, bring conviction, bring change, release judgment, enlighten, labor, plow, confirm, direct, uncover, dream, have visions, dance, edify, comfort, repair, heal, deliver, loose, bind, evangelize, shepherd, establish, set, unstop, charge, challenge, perfect, ordain, and encourage.

Some prophets are also scribes.

They write down their dreams, visions, prophetic words and insights. They love journaling (keeping a personal record of occurrences, experiences, and reflections kept on a regular basis; a diary).

> Therefore I send you prophets, and wise men, and scribes.
> —MATTHEW 23:34

The scribal prophet is not limited to writing, but can release the word through audio, video, print, and other media. They have a desire to record what God is saying.

> Scribal prophets are not simply prophets who write and record personal prophecy, or the occasional prophetic word. They are actually vessels that God uses fully as His prophets (in every sense of the word); but who also have a burning passion rooted inside them to record, watch over, release and teach the messages of heaven entrusted to them under a specific directive. (Read Ezekiel 9 and Ezekiel 10 in full.)[4]
> —THERESA HARVARD JOHNSON

Scribal prophets, go back and read the things you wrote down years ago, and you might be shocked at what the Lord has done to bring those words to pass. Some of you have journals that you have written over the years. God is faithful.

Scribes are also persecuted.

Religious systems of control hate scribes. This is because their writings challenge these systems. Truth and revelation can be imparted and released through writing. Writing has always been a powerful tool of reformation.

> Therefore I send you prophets, and wise men, and scribes. Some of them you will kill and crucify, and some you will scourge in your synagogues and persecute them from city to city.
>
> —MATTHEW 23:34

Prophet musicians

We need more than musicians. We need prophet musicians who release the sound of heaven on earth. Biblical examples of prophet musicians are Asaph, Heman, and Jeduthun.

> Then David and the officers of the army also set apart for the service some of the sons of Asaph, and of Heman, and of Jeduthun, those who prophesied with lyres, harps, and cymbals. The number of those who did the work according to their service was…
>
> —1 CHRONICLES 25:1

Heman, King David's seer

Heman was a musician and a seer. We need more than musicians. We need prophet (seer) musicians.

> All these were the sons of Heman, the king's seer, according to the words of God, to exalt him, for God gave fourteen sons and three daughters to Heman.
>
> —1 CHRONICLES 25:5

Singing prophets

John and Jesus ministered to Israel in different ways. Prophetic ministry is like a song. John came singing a dirge (a song of mourning). Jesus came playing a wedding song. Israel did not respond to either.

Prophets require a response. Prophets release a sound and a song. What are the prophets singing and playing?

> We piped to you [playing wedding], and you did not dance; we wailed dirges [playing funeral], and you did not mourn and beat your breasts and weep aloud.
>
> —MATTHEW 11:17, AMP

Dancing prophets

Both Miriam and David expressed themselves in the dance. Prophets are expressive, and the dance is one of the most powerful ways to express God's power, victory, love, and mercy.

> Miriam the prophetess, the sister of Aaron, took a timbrel in her hand, and all the women went out after her with timbrels and with dancing.
>
> —EXODUS 15:20

> David danced before the LORD with all of his might, and he wore a linen ephod.
>
> —2 SAMUEL 6:14

> They are like children sitting in the marketplace, calling to each other, saying: "We played the flute for you, and you did not dance; we mourned to you, and you did not weep."
>
> —LUKE 7:32

HOW PROPHETS OPERATE WITH OTHER MINISTRY GIFTS

Prophets and pastors

Prophets sometimes clash with pastors. Some pastors have a hard time dealing with prophets. Pastors need to be prophetic as well. Prophetic pastors will be better able to embrace prophets and prophetic people. One of the worst things that can happen to a prophet is to be shut down by pastors.

Controlling pastors don't like prophets. This is because control and domination are a form of witchcraft, and prophets can smell it out.

But these pastors should beware: when a church or denomination loses its prophets (they depart, get put out, or get shut down), it will begin to decline spiritually. Sometimes it is unnoticeable at first, but eventually the presence of God departs and it becomes a monument instead of a movement.

> Now the boy Samuel was ministering to the Lord before Eli. And the word of the Lord was rare in those days. There was no vision coming forth.
>
> —1 SAMUEL 3:1

Prophets and apostles

Prophets like being with apostles, and apostles like being with prophets. These two ministries are linked together in the New Testament. Prophets stir apostles, and apostles stir prophets. These ministries complement and strengthen each other. They both tend to be persecuted and misunderstood, and it seems as if they understand each other.

Prophets should be apostolic, and apostles should be prophetic.

> Therefore also the wisdom of God said, "I will send them prophets and apostles, and some of them they will kill and persecute."
>
> —LUKE 11:49

Many apostolic leaders are married to prophetic spouses.

Apostles and prophets work together. They complement and balance each other. Apostles tend to deal with structure and order, while prophets are more spontaneous. Apostles can become too rigid and need prophets to help them stay flexible and spontaneous. Prophets can be too spontaneous and need the order and structure of the apostle. These ministries can impart into each other and both be more balanced as a result.

Prophets and apostles are similar in their functions.

Many of the prophets in the Old Testament did what we would consider apostolic today. Many apostles today are doing what the Old Testament would consider prophetic. Jesus said He would send (which is the Greek word *apostolos*) prophets and apostles (Luke 11:49). Prophets therefore are sent (*apostolos*).

Prophets should be apostolic, that is, "sent ones." They should be sent with power and authority to establish and build.

Prophets and apostles work well together.

The apostle breaks and establishes new ground, biblical purpose, and order in enemy territory; and prophets bring fire, passion, and a continual sense of urgency into the faith communities of those entities established by apostles.[5]

The apostle needs the prophet to keep the fire burning in what has been pioneered and established.

Prophets and apostles working together results in synergy.

Synergy is the "interaction or cooperation of two or more organizations, substances, or other agents to produce a combined effect greater than the sum of their separate effects."[6] Apostolic leaders need prophetic input (both verbally and in anointing), or their churches will lack a fundamental ingredient needed to keep momentum. Prophets help release energy and enthusiasm.

Prophets and apostles want to see Christ formed in believers.

Prophets desire the image of Christ to be seen in the saints. This is the travail (labor, hardship, birthing…) of the prophet. This is also the desire and labor of apostles.

> My dear children, I am suffering the pains of giving birth
> to you all over again—and this will go on until the Messiah
> takes shape in you.
> —GALATIANS 4:19, CJB

Prophets and apostles hate when we glory in men.

There is nothing wrong with honoring men. There is nothing
wrong with supporting leaders. We are not to glory in them. *To glory*
means to boast. Apostles and prophets will challenge "boasting in
men." All the men and women God sends belong to us all.

> So let no one exult proudly concerning men [boasting of
> having this or that man as a leader], for all things are yours.
> —1 CORINTHIANS 3:21, AMP

God is not looking for super prophets and apostles.

You don't have to be an "elite" or "super" prophet to hear and speak
for the Lord. Don't compare yourselves with others. Many have elevated these ministries to a level where people feel they can never arrive.
There were hundreds of prophets in Israel whose names are never
mentioned in the Bible. Be you.

Prophets and evangelists

Together, prophets and evangelists, make sure the fire never goes
out. The fire of prayer, worship, and evangelism must never go out.
This fire must burn from generation to generation.

> A perpetual fire shall be kept burning on the altar. It shall
> never go out.
> —LEVITICUS 6:13

Prophets and teachers

These ministries work together to build the church. Prophets and
teachers complement each other. Prophets need teachers to help with
instruction. Teachers need prophets to help with inspiration. These
two working together balance each other and strengthen each other.
They also provide and atmosphere for apostolic release (Acts 13:1–5).

In the church that was in Antioch there were prophets and
teachers: Barnabas, Simeon who was called Niger, Lucius of
Cyrene, Manaen who had been brought up with Herod the
tetrarch, and Saul.

—ACTS 13:1

Prophets and other prophets

Prophets are not out of control when they minister. Prophets are
disciplined people who respect order (prophets hate disorder and confusion). Prophets know how to work with and minister with others,
especially other prophets.

Prophets are the hardest on each other. Prophets know other
prophets. Prophets can discern when something is wrong with
another prophet.

Let two or three prophets speak, and let the others judge.

—1 CORINTHIANS 14:29

The spirits of the prophets are subject to the prophets.

—1 CORINTHIANS 14:32

The spirits of prophets are under the control of [subject to]
the prophets themselves [unlike in pagan religions, where a
spirit would seize control of a speaker, causing frenzy, mania
or ecstasy].

—1 CORINTHIANS 14:32, EXB
(SEE ALSO 1 KINGS 18:28)

PROPHETIC WOMEN

There are many pastors who have prophetic wives. Some pastors want
their wives to be first ladies who simply look good and smile. Some
pastors do not receive the gift that God has placed in their wives
and do not allow them or release them to minister. This is shameful
and needs to stop. Don't allow religion and tradition to keep women
locked up in a box. God did not give women the Holy Ghost to sit
down, be quiet, and be stopped and ignored. Pastors like this will end

up in trouble because they reject the gift that God has placed in their lives to help.

Prophetic women will hit the nail on the head.

This is a prophetic word God gave me for women using the example of Jael driving a nail through the head of Sisera.

> Then Jael the wife of Heber took a tent peg and a hammer
> in her hand and went quietly to him, for he was fast asleep
> and tired. She drove the tent peg into his temple, and it went
> down into the ground, so he died.
>
> —Judges 4:21

Hit the nail on the head means to get to the precise point; do or say something exactly right; to be accurate; to hit the mark; to detect and expose (a lie, scandal, etc.).

Prophetic women, get ready to "hit the nail on the head." Your prophetic utterances will "hit the mark."

The daughters of Zelophehad

The daughters have an inheritance. The daughters have an inheritance in the prophetic ministry. The daughters also prophesy. Apostolic fathers release and bless the daughters.

> Then came near the daughters of Zelophehad, the son of
> Hepher, the son of Gilead, the son of Makir, the son of
> Manasseh, of the families of Manasseh the son of Joseph, and
> these are the names of his daughters: Mahlah, Noah, Hoglah,
> Milkah, and Tirzah. They stood before Moses, and before
> Eleazar the priest, and before the leaders and all the assembly
> by the door of the tent of meeting, saying, "Our father died
> in the wilderness, and he was not in the company of them
> that gathered against the LORD, in the company of Korah, but
> died in his own sin and had no sons. Why should the name of
> our father diminish from among his family, because he has no
> son? Give to us a possession among the brothers of our father."

Moses brought their case before the LORD. The Lord spoke to Moses, saying: The daughters of Zelophehad speak right. You will certainly give them an inheritance among their father's brothers, and you will cause the inheritance of their father to pass on to them.

—NUMBERS 27:1–7

Philip's daughters

Philip had four daughters who did prophesy (Acts 21:9). The prophet Joel said the daughters would prophesy (Joel 2:28). There were a number of women in the Upper Room (Acts 1:14). The release of the Holy Spirit on the Day of Pentecost opened the door for women to be involved in the prophetic ministry in an unprecedented way. Women are now released to prophesy in numbers that are greater than ever before.

> "In the last days it shall be," says God, "that I will pour out My Spirit on all flesh; your sons and your daughters shall prophesy, your young men shall see visions, and your old men shall dream dreams.

—ACTS 2:17

Miriam

Miriam, the sister of Moses, was a prophet. She led the women in dancing to celebrate God's victory over Pharaoh. She is also recognized as being sent along with Moses and Aaron to bring Israel out of Egypt. She therefore played a prominent role in Israel's deliverance from bondage.

> Miriam the prophetess, the sister of Aaron, took a timbrel in her hand, and all the women went out after her with timbrels and with dancing.

—EXODUS 15:20

For I have brought you up from the land of Egypt, and from the house of slaves I have redeemed you; and I sent before you Moses, Aaron, and Miriam.

—Micah 6:4

Huldah

Huldah was a prophet who was recognized by King Josiah. When the king discovered the Book of the Law, he rent his clothes and sent men to Huldah to inquire of the Lord. Huldah was the keeper of the king's wardrobe and spoke the word of the Lord to the king about the coming judgment upon Israel. She stated that it would not happen in his day because he had humbled himself.

"Go and seek the Lord on my behalf and on the behalf of the remnant in Israel and Judah concerning what is written in the book that was found, for the wrath of the Lord that is poured out on us is great because our fathers have not kept the word of the Lord, to do everything that is written in this book."

So Hilkiah and those with the king went to Huldah the prophetess, the wife of Shallum the son of Tokhath, son of Hasrah, who kept the wardrobe. She lived in Jerusalem in the Second Quarter, and they spoke to her about this.

And she said to them, "So says the Lord God of Israel: Speak to the man who sent you all to Me."

—2 Chronicles 34:21–23

Deborah

Deborah was a prophetess, a judge, and a mother in Israel. She was a national prophet and judge who was recognized throughout Israel. Israel came to her to settle disputes. Prophets can help settle disputes. Deborah's role as a mother represented her love and compassion for Israel. Mothers can be prophets.

Now Deborah, the wife of Lappidoth, was a prophetess. She judged Israel at that time.

—Judges 4:4

Village life ceased. It ceased until I, Deborah, arose; I arose
like a mother in Israel.

—JUDGES 5:7

Isaiah's wife

The major prophet Isaiah considered his wife to be a prophetess.
This shows that both a husband and wife can be prophets. This will
make a strong prophetic team.

So I went in to the prophetess, and she conceived and bore
a son. Then the LORD said to me, Call his name Maher-
Shalal-Hash-Baz.

—ISAIAH 8:3

Anna

Anna was a praying and fasting prophet. She spoke to all those
who were looking for redemption and the coming Messiah. By her
prayer and fasting, she helped prepare the way for the Lord to come.
She prayed and fasted in the temple and did not depart from the
house of God. Anna is a picture of the intercessory prophet.

And there was Anna a prophetess, a daughter of Phanuel, of
the tribe of Asher. She was of a great age and had lived with
her husband seven years from her virginity. And she was a
widow of about eighty-four years of age who did not depart
from the temple, but served God with fasting and prayer
night and day. Coming at that moment she gave thanks to
the Lord and spoke of Him to all those who looked for the
redemption of Jerusalem.

—LUKE 2:36–38

YOUNG PROPHETS

A young prophet was told to go to Bethel, cry out against the sin of
Israel, not remain, and return another way. An older prophet met him
and lied to him, telling him an angel had appeared, and said for him

to remain and eat at his house. The young prophet was deceived, ate with the old prophet, and was eaten by a lion.

Young prophet, be careful. Don't allow anyone, including another prophet, tell you something different from what God tells you.

The older prophet lied to him because he wanted the young prophet to eat with him at his house. He was probably lonely and was excited to see another prophet in Bethel.

> He said to him, "I am a prophet like you, and an angel spoke to me by the word of the Lord, saying, 'Bring him back with you into your house so that he may eat bread and drink water.'" But he had lied to him.
>
> —1 Kings 13:18

> As he was going, a lion met him on the way and killed him, and his body was thrown in the road, and both the donkey and lion stood by it. Some men passed by and saw the body thrown in the road with the lion standing by the body, and they came and told the story in the city where the old prophet lived.
>
> 1 Kings 13:24–25

Three things the Lord requires

These three things apply to all believers, and especially prophets. Young prophets, learn what the Lord requires of you and be faithful to do and say all He commands.

> He has told you, O man, what is good—and what does the Lord require of you, but to do justice and to love kindness, and to walk humbly with your God?
>
> —Micah 6:8

1. Do justly. Treat people fairly. Don't take advantage of the weak. Don't mistreat others. Don't use your power and authority to destroy others. Don't return evil for good. Don't forget or overlook people who helped you. Don't betray your friends. Don't use and misuse others for

personal gain. Don't destroy people through slander and backbiting. Protect and defend the innocent. Don't cheat people, but give everyone what is due to them. Issue correct verdicts and judgments against evil and wickedness. Don't favor or excuse the wicked and rebellious.

2. Love mercy. Be kind and compassionate to others. Show loving-kindness. Don't be critical, self-righteous, and condemning. Be forgiving and kind. Help and bless those who are oppressed. Support the weak. Be generous and benevolent. Bless those who curse you.

3. Walk humbly. Don't be vain, proud, rude, and arrogant. Don't look down upon others. Don't be self-promoting. Always be teachable. Be willing to receive correction. Admit when you are wrong, and be quick to apologize. Bow, worship, and always be reverent of God. Don't think of yourself more highly than you ought to think. Honor and respect those who are greater than you. Submit and respect those in authority. Don't forget where you came from. Examine yourself.

Maintaining an attitude of humility is essential in the prophetic ministry. Otherwise, elitism creeps in and grows up to characterize prophetic individuals and groups. Experiencing supernatural revelation can be "heady wine," and people too often begin to think of themselves more highly than they ought after having drunk it over a period of time.[7]

—MICHAEL SULLIVANT

Cultivate your gift.

Cultivating a prophetic life also includes cultivating a hidden life in the Word. Knowing the scriptures enables us to know the character of God, the way He speaks and the parameters He has laid out for prophetic ministry. We can judge prophecy through the standard of the Word and through the fruit of the Spirit knowing that we can discard any words we receive that don't line up with His scripture and the fruit of love, joy, peace, patience, kindness, goodness, faithfulness, gentleness and self-control.[8]

—Patricia Bootsma

The Unusual Life of a Prophet

Prophets can find themselves in the most unusual places and circumstances, and wonder, "How did I get here?" Prophet, God has a way of placing you there to release His wisdom and His word. Don't be surprised where you find yourself ministering. God will open doors for you, send you, and place you with people who you ordinarily would never meet. They need what you have.

> Arise, go to Zarephath, which belongs to Sidon, and live there. I have commanded a widow there to provide for you.
>
> —1 Kings 17:9

Your unusual assignments could have you ministering to presidents, government officials, businessmen, celebrities, widows, and more.

Prophets are often called to speak to power.

Prophets can speak to people of power and those in positions of power. This is because power is so easily abused and misused. Nathan spoke to David. This is an example of speaking to power. Sometimes power does not want to hear what prophets say. Jesus spoke to power when He challenged the religious leaders of His day for their hypocrisy and abuse.

> Ahab said to Elijah, "Have you found me, my enemy?" And he answered, "I have found you, because you have sold yourself to work evil in the sight of the Lord."
>
> —1 Kings 21:20

Prophets are called to speak to political power, economic power, religious power, and so on. Prophets also pray for those in power.

Power tends to corrupt, and absolute power corrupts absolutely. Great men are almost always bad men.[9]

—BARON ACTON

This famous quote addresses the fact that men have a difficult time handing power. Pride tends to corrupt men of power, and this is why we need prophets who will speak to and challenge power.

Moses is the exception. He was a man of great power, but he is called the meekest man of the earth. He never needed a prophet to correct him.

Now the man Moses was very humble, more than all the men on the face of the earth.

—NUMBERS 12:3

I will break the pride of your power; and I will make your heaven as iron, and your earth as brass.

—LEVITICUS 26:19

Prophets threaten religious position.

The Pharisees hated Jesus because they felt they would lose their place. This was the heart of the matter. They had worked years building their positions, and were afraid of losing those positions.

They hated Jesus not because He called them names, but because He threatened their security, prestige and income. He was going to ruin everything they had worked so hard for.[10]

—R. C. SPROUL JR.

If we leave Him alone like this, everyone will believe in Him, and the Romans will come and take away both our temple and our nation.

—JOHN 11:48

A prophet's gifts will work in the most unusual places.

Joseph's gift worked in the prison and took him to the palace. People need prophets everywhere. Those who need you will find you, or God will send you to them. Your gift will make room for you and bring you before great men (Prov. 18:16).

Prophets have unusual experiences with God (Peniel).

Prophets are not normal, and their experiences are not normal. Prophets are different because they have visitations. Unusual salvations, deliverances, dreams, visions, and divine encounters are the prophet's portion. When a person encounters God, they cannot remain the same.

Moses encountered a burning bush. Isaiah saw the Lord in His glory. Ezekiel had visions of God. Daniel had angelic visitations. Jeremiah encountered God at a young age. John was filled with the Holy Ghost from his mother's womb. God appeared to Jacob in a dream.

Prophets are different because they encounter God in unusual ways. Prophets have unusual testimonies. If you tell people some of your experiences, they might think you are crazy and spooky.

God deals with prophets at night.

It is not uncommon for God to deal with prophets in the night. Night visions, prayer in the night, and night meditations are common for many prophets.

> When I remember You on my bed, and meditate on You in the night watches.
>
> —Psalm 63:6

> May I remember my song in the night; may I meditate in my heart; my spirit made a diligent search.
>
> —Psalm 77:6

> Then the watchman called: "O Lord, I stand continually on the watchtower in the daytime, and I am stationed at my guard post every night."
>
> —Isaiah 21:8

I saw in the night visions, and there was one like a Son of Man
coming with the clouds of heaven. He came to the Ancient of
Days and was presented before Him.

—DANIEL 7:13

**The prophet's lifestyle is contrary to what they are speaking
against.**

There is a reason why John the Baptist was in the wilderness and not in Jerusalem, though he was the son of a priest.
He could not be where the Establishment was. He could not
enjoy its benefits and at the same time "blow the whistle" on
the falsity of it. We cannot in our own lifestyle indulge in the
very thing that we are condemning before others. Lifestyle
is, therefore, remarkably important with regard to the word
that is to be proclaimed and probably nothing more betrays
whether you are a true or false prophet than this.[11]

—ART KATZ

THE SECRET LIFE OF A PROPHET

Prophets do most of their work in secret. Prophets don't have to have
platforms, although God may give them one. Prophets don't have to
be seen, although God may highlight them. Prophets pray, weep, minister to the Lord, and study in secret. What God shows them in secret,
they speak to the world. Prophets love the solitary place. Prophets
hate the hype and sensationalism they see on many platforms.

Jesus prayed in secret.

In the morning, rising up a great while before sunrise, He
went out and departed to a solitary place. And there He
prayed.

—MARK 1:35

But you, when you pray, enter your closet, and when you have
shut your door, pray to your Father who is in secret. And your
Father who sees in secret will reward you openly.

—MATTHEW 6:6

Prophets weep in secret.

Prophets weep because of pride and rebellion. They weep when no
one is watching. They weep in their closets. They weep in their secret
places.

But if you will not listen to it, my soul will weep in secret
places for your pride; and my eyes will weep sorely and run
down with tears, because the flock of the LORD is carried
away captive.

—JEREMIAH 13:17

Leaders call prophets secretly.

This is true especially of leaders who are in trouble.

Then Zedekiah the king sent and took him out; and the king
asked him secretly in his house, and said, "Is there any word
from the LORD?" And Jeremiah said, "There is!" Then he said,
"You shall be delivered into the hand of the king of Babylon."

—JEREMIAH 37:17

There was a man of the Pharisees named Nicodemus, a ruler
of the Jews. He came to Jesus by night and said to Him,
"Rabbi, we know that You are a teacher who has come from
God. For no one can do these signs that You do unless God
is with him."

—JOHN 3:1–2

Prophets are the hidden ones.

Prophets are often hidden from view. They do much of their work
in the secret place. The hidden ones are the "secret ones," "the pre-
cious ones," "the treasured ones."

They have taken crafty counsel against thy people, and consulted against thy hidden ones.

—PSALM 83:3, KJV

THE PRAYER LIFE OF A PROPHET

Prayer, intercession, supplication, asking, seeking, knocking, pleading, requesting, calling on, crying out, without ceasing, standing in the gap, in the closet, in the secret place, in the spirit, watching, lifting up, agreement, burden, persevering, effectual, fervent, prevailing, wrestling, weeping, laboring, travailing, birthing, groaning—these are what make up the prayer life of a prophet. The prophetess Anna, as I mentioned earlier, is a picture of an intercessory prophet.

> An important part of the prophet's task is prayer. Because he knows the mind of the Lord, he is in a position to pray effectively. He has a clear picture of what God is doing, so he knows where prayer is needed most. The prophet watches over the word of the Lord and prays it into being. He must not rest until God has fulfilled His word (Isaiah 62:6).[12]
>
> —RON McKENZIE

> Prophetic intercession is a ministry of faith. We do not always know the reason for the prayer burden that the Holy Spirit gives us; neither do we always learn the outcome of our prayers. But we do know that God is faithful. And—that the greatest reward of prophetic intercession is intimacy with the Holy Spirit.[13]
>
> —HELEN CALDER

PLACES WHERE PROPHETS GROW AND FLOURISH

Prophetic families

God can raise up your children to be prophets. God called Jeremiah when he was a child. Prophetic children must be handled differently. They are not like every other child. They are unique and very sensitive to the Spirit of God and the spirit realm.

I raised up some of your sons as prophets, and some of your
young men as Nazirites. Is it not so, O children of Israel? says
the LORD.

—AMOS 2:11

But the LORD said to me, "Do not say, 'I am a youth.' For you
shall go everywhere that I send you, and whatever I command
you, you shall speak."

—JEREMIAH 1:7

Prophetic communities: a company of prophets

When they came to the hill, a group of prophets met him.
And the Spirit of God came upon him, and he prophesied
among them.

—1 SAMUEL 10:10

First Samuel 10:10 is the first mention of "a company (cord,
chain, or band) of prophets" (Nabhis). There were previously individual prophets. And on one occasion the seventy
elders prophesied (Numbers 11:25), and Moses said, "Would
God that all the Lord's people were prophets, and that the
Lord would put his Spirit upon them." But until the time of
Samuel there was no association or community, college or
school, of prophets.

[The prophet Samuel's] language shows his intimate
relation to this "company," of which he was doubtless the
founder...Its formation was due to a newly awakened religious life among the people, and intended as a means of deep-
ening and extending it.

[The company] arose about the same time as the establishment of the monarchy, and furnished a regular succession of
prophets, by whom the word of the Lord was spoken for the
guidance and restraint of the king. "Samuel saw the need of
providing a new system of training for those who should be
his successors in the prophetic office, and formed into fixed

societies the sharers of the mystic gift, which was plainly capable of cultivation and enlargement."

They formed a "company," a voluntary, organised society, apparently dwelling together in the same place, and pursuing the same mode of life. The bond of their union was the common spirit they possessed; and their association contributed to their preservation and prosperity... "They presented the unifying, associative power of the prophetic spirit over against the disruption of the theocratic life, which was a legacy of the time of the judges" (Erdmann).[14]

This community of prophets was also active at the time of Elijah and Elisha. These companies consisted of women as well, such as Huldah the prophetess in 2 Kings 22:14:

So Hilkiah the priest, Ahikam, Akbor, Shaphan, and Asaiah went to Huldah the prophetess, wife of Shallum, son of Tikvah, son of Harhas, keeper of the wardrobe (she lived in Jerusalem in the second quarter), and they spoke with her.

These prophets came together in community to encourage each other and build up their gifts. They worshipped together, ate together, and sometimes lived together. The strength of their gifts did not develop in a vacuum. They were nurtured and confirmed by other like-minded people.

Let there be companies (groups) of prophets in every city and church. Prophet, you are not alone.

Then Saul sent messengers to take David, but when they saw the company of the prophets prophesying and Samuel taking his stand over them, the Spirit of God came upon the messengers of Saul and they also prophesied.

—1 SAMUEL 19:20

Prophetic houses

Strong prophetic churches will activate and release large numbers of prophets and prophetic people because of a strong prophetic atmosphere that is conducive to nurturing and developing prophets. Every city and region needs these kinds of churches to be established in order for the territory to receive the blessing of prophets and prophetic utterances. These churches will be strong in worship and prophecy, and have strong prophetic leaders to help mature emerging prophetic gifts. We are seeing more and more of these kinds of churches being established around the globe.

Prophets need a loving faith community where they are embraced, trained, and released. This is an atmosphere conducive to their growth and development. (See 1 Samuel 19:20.)

Prophetic hubs

Many churches will become prophetic hubs for their cities and regions. A hub is a center of activity or interest; a focal point; a center around which other things revolve or from which they radiate. These hubs will be places of encouragement, training, activation, and impartation for prophets and prophetic people. Ramah was a prophetic hub under the leadership of Samuel (1 Sam. 19:18–20).

Pray for these hubs to be established in your region. Find a hub to be encouraged and released into the prophetic flow.

> Now David fled, and he escaped and came to Samuel at Ramah. And he reported to him all that Saul had done to him. And he and Samuel went and stayed in Naioth. It was told Saul, saying, "David is at Naioth in Ramah."
> —1 SAMUEL 19:18–19

Prophetic teams

When people flow together in prophetic teams, it is easy to stir up and flow in prophecy. There is the prophetic influence that is established over the team, so that each finds it easy to

release prophecy. Also, each one adds to the flow and experience of the prophetic.[15]

—Ashish Raichur

Prophetic teams are good in helping young prophetic ministries
work with more experienced prophetic ministers. This helps younger
ministers develop and become stronger by being around those who
are more mature and stronger. There is also an impartation that can
be received, and valuable experience that helps people develop faith in
ministering prophetically.

School of the prophets

It was under the administration of the Prophet/Judge Samuel,
that we find the development of the school of the prophets.
In this particular time period, about 1050–931 B.C., there
were many false prophets that arose with false mediums of
revelation. Samuel, who was raised as a boy by a priest named
Eli, established training centers where young men would be
taught the Law of Moses, responding to the Spirit of God
and worship.

While one cannot be taught how to prophesy, the schools
were geared to instruct the sons of the prophets how to flow
with the Spirit when He came [upon] them.[16]

Prophetic caves

The church needs more Obadiah-type leaders. Obadiah protected,
fed, and sheltered the prophets in caves when Jezebel was trying to
destroy them. Some churches will have leaders with this Obadiah-
type anointing, and they will become prophetic caves to hide, shelter,
nourish, and protect prophets.

When Jezebel killed the prophets of the Lord, Obadiah took
a hundred prophets and hid them in groups of fifty in a cave
and fed them with bread and water.

—1 Kings 18:4

Prophetic wildernesses

Many prophets are developed in the wilderness because there is no place of development in the church. John was developed in the wilderness. There was no place for him to be developed in the religious system of Jerusalem.

> In those days John the Baptist came, preaching in the wilderness of Judaea.
>
> —MATTHEW 3:1

Prophetstown

I drove from Illinois to Iowa some time ago and passed a town by the name of Prophetstown in Illinois. I have lived in Illinois all my life, and I have never heard of this town. I researched it, and this is what I found:

> Prophetstown is named for Wabokieshiek (White Cloud) a medicine man known as "the Prophet." [He was] also friend and adviser to Chief Black Hawk. Born in 1794 he presided over the village known as "prophet's village" on the Rock River. He was half Winnebago (Ho-Chunk) and half Sauk and had great influence over both tribes.[17]

I pray that the Lord would raise up "Prophetstowns" in every region across the globe. Let true prophets arise and come forth in every town and city. Let the Cloud of Glory (White Cloud) be in these towns.

> He said to him, "Look, there is in this city a man of God, and he is highly respected. All that he speaks surely comes about. Now let us go there. Perhaps he can show us the way that we should go."
>
> —1 SAMUEL 9:6

TO THE PROPHETS WHO ARE THE FIRSTS IN THEIR FAMILIES

Some prophets have prophets in their families. Some are the sons and daughters of prophets. But there is a prophet whom I love. These are the prophets who are the first in their families. God calls them and raises them up from nowhere. They have no prophetic legacy. They just seem to arrive on the scene as Amos did. They are pioneering prophets. They are not professional prophets. They are often trained directly by God.

> But Amos answered Amaziah: "I am no prophet, and I am no prophet's disciple. Rather, I am a herdsman and a dresser of sycamore trees. But the LORD took me away from the flock, and the LORD said to me, 'Go, prophesy to My people Israel.'"
>
> —AMOS 7:14–15

2

CHARACTERISTICS OF A PROPHET

The spirits of the prophets are subject to the prophets.

—1 CORINTHIANS 14:32

P ROPHETS ARE THE same all over the world. Although prophets can be different, they tend to have the same characteristics. Every nation has them. Every city has them. Every region has them. They exist in every generation. You are not alone. You are a part of a global company of prophets. The same things grieve them, stir them, give them joy, and cause them to weep. The following pages of this chapter list, identify, and describe common characteristics prophets share. This knowledge will give you strength and confidence to be the prophet God has called you to be and to recognize and validate the other prophets in your life.

Prophets are fiercely loyal to God and love justice.

Prophets have a fierce loyalty to God, and a love for justice (just behavior or treatment of others, especially the poor and disadvantaged). There is nothing wrong with you if injustice and mistreatment of others grieves and angers you. This is the way you are configured by God.

> No one calls for justice, nor does anyone plead for truth. They trust in vanity and speak lies; they conceive mischief and bring forth iniquity.
>
> —ISAIAH 59:4

> To do justice and judgment is more acceptable to the LORD than sacrifice.
>
> —PROVERBS 21:3

Prophets defend the poor, needy, and fatherless

It is the nature of a prophet to defend the poor and needy. Prophets hate injustice and will defend those who are being treated unfairly.

> How long will ye judge unjustly, and accept the persons of the wicked? Selah. Defend the poor and fatherless: do justice to the afflicted and needy. Deliver the poor and needy: rid them out of the hand of the wicked.
> —PSALM 82:2–4, KJV

Prophets cry out for justice and fairness.

Righteousness can be translated as justice, fairness, and equity. The prophets hated religion and sacrifice without justice and fairness.

> But let justice and fairness flow like a river that never runs dry.
> —AMOS 5:24, CEV

> But let justice run down like water, and righteousness like an ever-flowing stream.
> —AMOS 5:24

> Then you will understand righteousness and judgment and equity, and every good path.
> —PROVERBS 2:9

Justice was a major theme of the prophets. The prophets equated justice with righteousness. You cannot be unjust and righteous at the same time. Synonyms for *justice* include equitability, equitableness, evenhandedness, fair-mindedness, fairness, impartiality; goodness, righteousness, virtue; honor, integrity, uprightness.

The opposite words for justice include bias, favor, favoritism, non-objectivity, one-sidedness, partiality, partisanship, prejudice.

Prophets deal with injustice.

The story of Naboth highlights how prophets deal with injustice. Jezebel took possession of Naboth's vineyard for Ahab by setting up false witnesses and having him killed. This is an example of the powerful taking advantage of the weak. God sent a word through Elijah to Ahab that the dogs would lick his blood in the place where they licked Naboth's blood.

> You shall speak to him, saying, "Thus says the LORD: Have you killed and also taken possession?" And you shall speak to him, saying, "Thus says the LORD: In the place where dogs licked the blood of Naboth, dogs will lick your own blood!"
>
> —1 KINGS 21:19

Another illustration of how prophets deal with injustice is found in the Bible where David took Bathsheba, Uriah's wife, and had Uriah killed. Nathan came to David and exposed this injustice. David had many flocks and herds but took from Uriah the only lamb he had. This is another example of the strong taking advantage of the weak. This was a grave injustice.

> The LORD sent Nathan to David…Then Nathan told David, "You are this man! Thus says the LORD, the God of Israel: I anointed you as king over Israel and I rescued you from the hand of Saul. I gave to you your master's house and your master's wives into your arms, and I gave to you the house of Israel and Judah. If this were too little, I would have continued to do for you much more. Why have you despised the word of the LORD by doing evil in His sight? You struck down Uriah the Hittite with the sword, and you took his wife as a wife for yourself. You killed him with the sword of the Ammonites. Now the sword will never depart from your house, because you have despised Me and have taken the wife of Uriah the Hittite to be your wife."
>
> —2 SAMUEL 12:1–10

Prophets will not gloss over injustice or oppression.

A prophetic voice…will not be silent in the face of bigotry or prejudice or false pride, and will not compromise faithfulness for practical ends no matter how noble those ends may be in themselves. A truly prophetic voice is one that will sweep away all the trappings of religion and simply ask, "What does God require?", and answer simply, "do justice, love mercy, walk humbly with God." Or simply "love God, love others." A prophetic voice is one that will settle for nothing less than holiness of heart and life as the result of faithful obedience to the voice of God. In a real sense, a prophetic voice even today is the voice of God.[1]

—DENNIS BRATCHER

Prophets will take a stand.

Prophets will stand up against the workers of iniquity when no one else will. Prophets will answer the call and rise against evildoers.

> Who will rise up for me against the wicked? Who will stand up for me against those who do iniquity?

—PSALM 94:16

Prophets are different.

Prophets are not normal. Prophets are different. They are configured differently. They don't think like everyone else. They see things differently. They do not like people saying, "This is just the way it is," or "We have always done it this way."

They see what others do not see. They are not satisfied with the status quo. They see God's agenda of advancement and change. They desire new moves and new things. They often have a holy discontent. Prophets are change agents.

If this is you, then you are not alone. Prophets are the same everywhere, in every nation. There are many just like you. You are not crazy, and you are not alone.

> Still, I have preserved seven thousand men in Israel for Myself, all of whose knees have not bowed to Baal and whose mouths have not kissed him.

—1 KINGS 19:18

Prophets march to the beat of a different drummer.

Prophets are motivated by a different set of values than the average person.

Prophets are motivated by love.

They have a love for God, His people (the church), and the world. They will stand against anything that comes to kill, steal, and destroy. This love makes them protectors, defenders, deliverers, and intercessors.

The core message of a prophet
Love God, and love one another…
Prophets will deal with anything that keeps us from loving God and from loving one another.

> Jesus said to him, "'You shall love the Lord your God with all your heart, and with all your soul, and with all your mind.' This is the first and great commandment. And the second is like it: 'You shall love your neighbor as yourself.'"
>
> —MATTHEW 22:37–39

Prophets extend mercy.

Sometimes prophets are portrayed as only being harsh and mean, but prophets are merciful. Prophets are uncompromising, but there is room for mercy and redemption in their messages. Prophets represent the heart of God, and God is merciful.

> It is of the LORD's mercies that we are not consumed; His compassions do not fail.
>
> —LAMENTATIONS 3:22

> Go and proclaim these words toward the north, and say: Return, backsliding Israel, says the LORD, and I will not cause My anger to fall on you. For I am merciful, says the LORD, and I will not keep anger forever.
>
> —JEREMIAH 3:12

In a little wrath I hid My face from you for a moment; but
with everlasting kindness I will have mercy on you, says the
LORD your Redeemer.

—ISAIAH 54:8

Prophets see the potential in small things.

Prophets can see the beginning, and where a thing is going. They
can see potential when others see smallness.

For who has despised the day of small things? These seven
will rejoice and see the plumb line in the hand of Zerubbabel.
These are the eyes of the LORD, which survey to and fro
throughout the earth.

—ZECHARIAH 4:10

Prophets are seers.

Prophets see what is hidden from most. They discern when things
are not right and out of order. They often wonder why everyone does
not see it. They often think, "Am I crazy? Am I really seeing this?"
Prophets hate spiritual blindness. They are grieved when leaders and
believers cannot see what is so obvious to them. Some people see what
they want to see, and some don't see what they don't want to see, but
the prophet can't help but to see.

Be encouraged, prophets. There are many seeing the same thing
you are seeing. There are many praying about the same things. You
are not crazy, and you are not alone.

Prophets see thing from heaven's perspective.

Prophets say to us, "Come up higher."

After this I looked. And there was an open door in heaven.
The first voice I heard was like a trumpet speaking with me,
saying, "Come up here, and I will show you things which
must take place after this."

—REVELATION 4:1

Prophets access God's thoughts.

Prophets know what God is thinking, and they speak what God is thinking. God's thoughts are not man's thoughts. Prophets think differently. Prophets are not limited to the way that men think.

> For My thoughts are not your thoughts, nor are your ways My ways, says the LORD. For as the heavens are higher than the earth, so are My ways higher than your ways, and My thoughts than your thoughts.
>
> —ISAIAH 55:8–9

Prophets know God's ways.

Israel knew the acts of God, but Moses knew His ways. The Amplified Version says, "He made known His ways [of righteousness and justice] to Moses, His acts to the people of Israel" (Ps. 103:7). It is not enough to know the acts of God; we must also know His ways.

Prophets wait on the Lord.

They have an expectation of what the Lord will do. They wait for Him to act. They wait for Him to judge. They wait for Him to reveal Himself. They wait for Him to fulfill His word.

> My soul waits for the Lord, more than watchmen for the morning, more than watchmen for the morning.
>
> —PSALM 130:6

> I will wait on the LORD, who hides His face from the house of Jacob, and I will eagerly look for Him.
>
> —ISAIAH 8:17

Prophets ask the hard questions.

Prophets want to know why. They desire insight and understanding when life seems confusing. They don't settle for the religious saying, "You never can really know the mind of God." The prophet is God's friend. They want insight into perplexing questions and challenges in their generation and society.

I will stand at my watch and station myself on the watch-tower; and I will keep watch to see what He will say to me, and what I will answer when I am reproved. And the LORD answered me: Write the vision, and make it plain on tab-lets, that he who reads it may run. For the vision is yet for an appointed time; but it speaks of the end, and does not lie. If it delays, wait for it; it will surely come, it will not delay.

—HABAKKUK 2:1–3

Prophets ask, "Who has bewitched You?"

Who has bewitched you that you should not obey the truth? Before your eyes Jesus Christ was clearly portrayed among you as crucified?

—GALATIANS 3:1

The Galatians had been bewitched by legalistic teachers. The Amplified Version says, "Who has fascinated or bewitched or cast a spell over you?" Another translation says, "Who has hypnotized you?"

Prophets oppose the wisdom of the world.

The church cannot operate in worldly wisdom but in godly wisdom. God's wisdom is higher than man's, whose wisdom is earthly, sensual, and devilish.

Therefore I will once again do a marvelous work among this people, even a marvelous work and a wonder; for the wisdom of their wise men shall perish, and the understanding of their prudent men shall be hidden.

—ISAIAH 29:14

Where is the wise? Where is the scribe? Where is the debater of this age? Has God not made the wisdom of this world foolish?

—1 CORINTHIANS 1:20

Prophets uproot what God has not planted.

> But He answered, "Every plant which My heavenly Father has not planted will be uprooted."
>
> —Matthew 15:13

Prophets are used by God to release other people into their assignments and destinies.

Prophets know the people whom God has called and appointed. They know the ones who are called and the ones who are not called. They love to see people released into their purposes. Prophets are not selfish. They want to see others fulfill their purposes.

> And the Lord said to him, Go, return on the road through the Wilderness of Damascus, and when you arrive, anoint Hazael to be king over Aram.
>
> —1 Kings 19:15

Prophets are midwives.

Midwives assist in delivery. Prophets assist us in bringing forth the plans of God for our lives through prayer, preaching, teaching, and prophesying—birthing.

> Because the midwives feared God, He gave them families.
>
> —Exodus 1:21

Prophets are inspired.

Prophets are moved by inspiration. Once they get inspired to do something, they are hard to stop. Once they get stirred up, watch out. They will fight through every obstacle once they know something is of God. Don't underestimate the power of inspiration.

Prophets know the power of inspiration.

Inspiration is the process of being stimulated to do or feel something, especially to do something creative. Prophets are...

+ Inspired to speak
+ Inspired to pray

+ Inspired to sing
+ Inspired to worship

Prophets are feared.

Herod was afraid of John. God uses prophets to release a holy fear. Holy fear is needed today. Let the prophets arise and bring a holy fear to this generation.

> For Herod feared John, knowing that he was a righteous and holy man, and protected him. When he heard him, he was greatly perplexed, but heard him gladly.
>
> —MARK 6:20

Prophets call out sin.

God has always used prophets to call out sin.

> Cry aloud, do not hold back; lift up your voice like a trumpet, and show My people their transgression and the house of Jacob their sins.
>
> —ISAIAH 58:1

> If I had not come and spoken to them, they would not have had sin. But now they have no excuse for their sin.
>
> —JOHN 15:22

Prophets fight carnality.

Carnality has always been a problem with churches. *Carnal* means to be fleshly or worldly. Prophets will oppose it. Carnality results in being sectarian and exalting of men. Carnality includes envy, strife, division.

> And I, brethren, could not speak unto you as unto spiritual, but as unto carnal, even as unto babes in Christ. I have fed you with milk, and not with meat: for hitherto ye were not able to bear it, neither yet now are ye able. For ye are yet carnal: for whereas there is among you envying, and strife, and divisions, are ye not carnal, and walk as men?
>
> —1 CORINTHIANS 3:1–3, KJV

Prophets call for fasting, prayer, and humility.

Prophets often call the church to humility. Repentance from pride, disobedience, and rebellion is needed. Fasting is one of the biblical ways to humble the soul. Humility, repentance, and fasting are keys to breakthrough.

> Consecrate a fast, call a sacred assembly, assemble the elders and all the inhabitants of the land to the house of the LORD your God, and cry out to the LORD.
>
> —JOEL 1:14

> Yet even now, declares the LORD, return to Me with all your heart, and with fasting and with weeping and with mourning....Blow the ram's horn in Zion, consecrate a fast, call a solemn assembly.
>
> —JOEL 2:12, 15

Prophets offend people.

People can be offended at prophets. Prophets can rub people the wrong way. Some people hate truth. They don't like what prophets say. Jesus offended the people in His hometown.

Jesus offended the Pharisees and the religious leaders of His day. He did not "butter them up," but He spoke the truth.

If you don't want to offend anyone, you cannot be a prophet.

> And they took offense at Him. But Jesus said to them, "A prophet is not without honor except in his own country and in his own house."
>
> —MATTHEW 13:57

> Then His disciples came and said to Him, "Do You know that the Pharisees were offended after they heard this saying?"
>
> —MATTHEW 15:12

Prophets speak what some people do not want to hear.

> And the king of Israel said to Jehoshaphat, "There is still one man, Micaiah the son of Imlah, by whom we can inquire of

the LORD. But I hate him because he never prophesies good
for me, but always evil." And Jehoshaphat said, "Let not the
king say so."

—1 KINGS 22:8

Prophets tell the truth.

Israel went into captivity because of bad prophetics (false and vain
prophets). These so-called prophets did not tell Israel the truth. Jeremiah stood against them and told Israel the truth. Tell the truth,
prophets.

> Your prophets have seen for you false and deceptive visions;
> they have not revealed your iniquity, to bring back your
> captives, but have seen for you oracles that are false and
> misleading.
>
> —LAMENTATIONS 2:14

Prophets are fervent.

Fervent means "having or showing great emotion or zeal; ardent;
very hot, glowing." Prophets are sometimes called "too emotional" or
"too zealous," but it is the nature of prophets to be fervent.

Fervent in prayer, love, preaching, teaching, and worship, they
often wonder why everyone is not fervent.

> Confess your faults to one another and pray for one another,
> that you may be healed. The effective, fervent prayer of a righ-
> teous man accomplishes much.
>
> —JAMES 5:16

> Epaphras greets you. He is one of you, a servant of Christ,
> always laboring fervently for you in prayers, that you may
> stand mature and complete in the entire will of God.
>
> —COLOSSIANS 4:12

> Above all things, have unfailing love for one another, because
> love covers a multitude of sins.
>
> —1 PETER 4:8

Prophets have zeal.

Zeal is passion and jealousy. Jesus had zeal for the house of God. This zeal caused Him to drive the moneychangers from the temple.

The house of God is the church. Prophets have a zeal (passion, jealousy) for the church. Zeal will consume prophets. They cannot sit by and watch the house of God be destroyed. They must act.

> My strong love [jealousy; passion; zeal] for your Temple [house] completely controls [consumes] me [John 2:17]. When people insult you, it hurts me [The reproaches/scorn of those who reproach/scorn you fall on me; Rom. 15:3].
>
> —PSALM 69:9, EXB

Prophets are radical.

The word *radical* means "departing markedly from the usual or customary; extreme or drastic."

Prophets can be set like flint.

A prophet will set his or her face like flint when they know something is of God. They will stand against the world if they have to. Flint is a very hard stone that symbolizes being set and unchangeable. Prophets take a stand with the help of God.

> For the Lord GOD will help me; therefore, I shall not be disgraced; therefore, I have set my face like a flint, and I know that I shall not be ashamed.
>
> —ISAIAH 50:7

Prophets need to understand when things don't make sense.

This can be very frustrating to a prophet. A prophet likes to make sense of things. They want to know why.

Prophets are sometimes too hard on themselves.

Prophets can be hard on themselves because of the nature of their gift. For this reason, it is sometimes difficult to restore a prophet when they fail.

Prophets are as open about their own failures as they want others to be about theirs.

Sometimes prophets can be too hard on themselves because of the way they view things. Don't come down too hard on yourself, prophet, if you make a mistake. There is room for mercy on others as well as yourself.

Prophets tend to be intense.

Prophets are not laid back. They have a difficult time under-standing believers who have no intensity. *Intense* means having or showing strong feelings or opinions; extremely earnest or serious.

Prophets are human.

Prophets are subject to like passions as others, yet they walk in power and authority by God's grace and calling. They don't allow their passions to stop them from doing what needs to be done. They've learned how to bring their passions under the rule of God and submit to His will. They pray harder.

> Elijah was a man subject to natural passions as we are, and he prayed earnestly that it might not rain, and it did not rain on the earth for three years and six months.
>
> —JAMES 5:17

Prophets are tenacious in prayer.

Once prophets get a burden, they will pray it through, no matter how long it takes. They will hold on to a prayer assignment for years if they have to. If you want a strong prayer ministry in your church, get some prophets together.

When prophets get a burden, they cannot shake it. They carry that burden. That burden is their assignment from the Lord. They try sometimes to shake it, but it will not leave them. You might as well deal with the burden, because it is not going anywhere. A burden is a weight, something the prophet carries. It can be a message, a ministry, or an assignment.

> The burden which Habakkuk the prophet did see.
>
> —Habakkuk 1:1, kjv

Prophets don't mind holy interruptions.

Prophets love it when God interrupts a service and does something new. Prophets get bored with routine and tradition. They don't like being stuck to an "order of service." They love the "suddenlies" of God.

> And suddenly there came a sound from heaven as of a rushing mighty wind, and it filled all the house where they were sitting.
>
> —Acts 2:2

God does some things suddenly. Sometimes what prophets speak "tarries," but other times it comes "suddenly."

Prophets are sensitive to the spirit realm.

Prophets are the most sensitive of the fivefold ministry. God has configured prophets to have spiritual sensitivity. Prophets have to learn how to handle this increased sensitivity. Prophets tend to "pick up things" without trying to. Their sensitivity is related to being extremely intuitive, highly aware, and keenly observant.

Prophets move in the spirit.

Immediately in the Spirit…

Carried away in the Spirit…

Pray in the Spirit…

Sing in the Spirit…

Walk in the Spirit…

Dance in the Spirit…

> The hand of the Lord was upon me, and He carried me out in the Spirit of the Lord and set me down in the midst of the valley which was full of bones.
>
> —Ezekiel 37:1

I was in the Spirit on the Lord's Day, and I heard behind me
a great voice like a trumpet.

—Revelation 1:10

Immediately I was in the Spirit. And there was a throne set in
heaven with One sitting on the throne!

—Revelation 4:2

And he carried me away in the spirit to a great and high mountain, and shewed me the Holy City, Jerusalem, descending out
of heaven from God.

—Revelation 21:10

Prophets are spontaneous.

Spontaneity is the result of inspiration. *Spontaneous* means "per-
formed or occurring as a result of a sudden inner impulse or inclina-
tion" and "without premeditation or external stimulus." Sometimes
churches don't care much for spontaneity. Some want everything pre-
planned.

Prophets expect new bottles and new wine.

And it will be that in that day the mountains will drip sweet
wine, and the hills will flow with milk, and all the streambeds
of Judah will flow with water; a spring will proceed from the
house of the Lord and will water the Valley of Shittim.

—Joel 3:18

But new wine must be put into new wineskins, and both are
preserved.

—Luke 5:38

Prophets smell uncleanness.

Did you know that prophets can smell? They can smell uncleanness. They can smell sin. They can also smell the sweet aroma of prayer
and worship. They can smell bread where the Word is preached. They
can smell the fragrance of the Lord when He is present in a church.

Prophet, don't be afraid to smell; you are not crazy.

If the whole body were an eye, where were the hearing? If the whole were hearing, where would the sense of smell be?

—1 CORINTHIANS 12:17

I rose up to open to my beloved, and my hands dripped with myrrh, my fingers with liquid myrrh on the handles of the bolt.

—SONG OF SONGS 5:5

Prophets know Jezebel.

Jezebel is a false prophetess. Elijah knew Jezebel, and Jezebel knew Elijah. Prophets hate when Jezebel is allowed to run rampant in the church. Jezebel represents a spirit of control, manipulation, seduction, intimidation, whoredom…

But I have a few things against you: You permit that woman Jezebel, who calls herself a prophetess, to teach and seduce My servants to commit sexual immorality and eat food sacrificed to idols.

—REVELATION 2:20

When Joram saw Jehu he said, "Is it peace, Jehu?" And he said, "What peace, so long as the harlotries of your mother Jezebel and her sorceries are so many?"

—2 KINGS 9:22

Prophets cry out against abominations.

An abomination is that which is disgusting and detestable. Here is what is abominable to God: pride, lying, murder, evil imaginations, mischief, false witness, and discord.

These six things the Lord hates, yes, seven are an abomination to him: a proud look, a lying tongue, and hands that shed innocent blood, a heart that devises wicked imaginations, feet that are swift in running to mischief, a false witness who speaks lies, and he who sows discord among brethren.

—PROVERBS 6:16–19

For the sons of Judah have done evil in My sight, says the
LORD. They have set their abominations in the house which
is called by My name, to pollute it.

—JEREMIAH 7:30

Prophets detect when thing are out of order.

They discern when situations are incased in disorder and confusion, or when there is misalignment.

For this reason I left you in Crete, that you should set in
order the things that are lacking, and appoint elders in every
city, as I commanded you.

—TITUS 1:5

For though I am absent in the flesh, yet I am with you in
spirit, rejoicing and seeing your orderliness and the steadfastness of your faith in Christ.

—COLOSSIANS 2:5

We have diverse gifts according to the grace that is given to
us: if prophecy, according to the proportion of faith.

—ROMANS 12:6

Prophets are not impressed with buildings.

Prophets are not impressed with religious adornment. They
understand that God does not dwell in temples made with hands.
They look for the true temple, which is the people of God filled with
the Holy Spirit.

However, the Most High does not dwell in houses made with
hands. As the prophet says…

—ACTS 7:48

As some spoke of how the temple was adorned with beautiful
stones and gifts, He said, "As for these things which you see,
the days will come when not one stone shall be left on another
that will not be thrown down."

—LUKE 21:5–6

Prophets are contagious.

Get around prophets and you will start being prophetic. The prophet's spirit is strong and influences others. God has called prophets to be contagious. You cannot keep this to yourself. You are an influencer. You can impart.

> After that you will come to the hill of God, where the garrison of the Philistines is. And when you come there to the city, you will meet a group of prophets coming down from the high place with a harp, a tambourine, a flute, and a lyre before them. And they will prophesy. And the Spirit of the Lord will come upon you, and you will prophesy with them. And you will be turned into another man.
>
> —1 Samuel 10:5–6

Prophets should want everyone to hear from and speak for God. Prophets should not want the prophetic to be a club for a few "anointed" people. Prophets want the leaders to be prophetic and the people to be prophetic. Prophets love it when people hear, speak, and obey the word of the Lord. Prophets are not jealous when God uses other people.

Sometimes when you ask a prophet, "What is God saying?," they will answer, "What is God saying to you?"

> Moses said to him, "Are you jealous for my sake? Oh, that all the people of the Lord were prophets, and that the Lord would put His Spirit upon them!"
>
> —Numbers 11:29

Prophets are concerned about God's agenda, purposes, and plans.

God's agenda is the priority of the prophet, not the agenda of man. The prophet knows that only the plans and purposes of the Lord will stand, and anything else is a waste of time. Prophets don't like to waste time on things that are not ordained by God.

Many plans are in a man's mind, but it is the Lord's purpose
for him that will stand.

—Proverbs 19:21, amp

Jesus said to them, "My food is to do the will of Him who
sent Me, and to finish His work.

—John 4:34

The Lord of Hosts has sworn, saying: Surely as I have
thought, so shall it come to pass, and as I have purposed, so
shall it stand.

—Isaiah 14:24

Prophets listen for a sound.

Sounds are important to prophets. The prophet's ears are opened
to the sounds of heaven. Certain sounds stir prophets. Anointed
music stirs prophets. The wrong sound is a sign that something is
wrong. Some churches and ministries have an old sound.

Elijah said to Ahab, "Get up, eat and drink, for there is a
sound of a heavy rainfall."

—1 Kings 18:41

Hear attentively the thunder of His voice, and the sound that
goes out of His mouth.

—Job 37:2

The clouds poured out water; the skies thundered. Your
arrows flashed about.

—Psalm 77:17

Here are examples of sounds that stir prophets:

+ Sound of the trumpet
+ Sound of many waters
+ Sound of rain
+ Sound of the alarm
+ Sound of wind
+ Sound of battle
+ Sound of shouting

+ Sound of praise
+ Sound of music
+ Sound of preaching
+ Sound of singing

Prophets are great helpers.

Prophets help build. They help leaders. They help churches. They help in prayer. They help in worship. They help us transition. They help us move into the new. It is the nature of a prophet to be a helper and have a desire to help. Prophets provide supernatural assistance. If you need help, get a prophet.

> Then Zerubbabel the son of Shealtiel and Joshua the son of Jozadak rose up and began to build the house of God which is at Jerusalem, and the prophets of God were with them, helping them.
>
> —Ezra 5:2

Prophets step up in a crises.

When others run from crisis, prophets step up. They are built and designed to bring solutions and order when there is crisis and chaos.

Prophets release courage.

Courage is important, especially for leaders. Asa took courage after he heard the word of Oded the prophet. He then pressed forward in removing the idols from the land. Prophets will encourage leaders to do what God desires.

> And when Asa heard these words of the prophecy of Azariah son of Oded the prophet, he was encouraged and removed the detestable idols from the entire land of Judah and Benjamin and from the cities that he captured in the hills of Ephraim. And he repaired the altar of the Lord that was before the vestibule of the Lord.
>
> —2 Chronicles 15:8

Prophets speak peace.

Shalom is the Hebrew word for peace, healing, wholeness, and prosperity.

> I will hear what God the LORD will speak, for He will speak peace to His people and to His saints, but let them not turn again to folly.
>
> —PSALM 85:8

Prophets speak to the gods.

The gods are the judges, the mighty, and the rulers. God stands in the congregation of the gods. We are the assembly of the gods (the rulers, the mighty, the sons and daughters of God). We are the judges, and God is in our midst. We issue verdicts and pass sentences. Rise up saints; you are the gods.

> God stands among the divine council; He renders judgment among the gods.
>
> —PSALM 82:1

> Elohim [God] stands in the divine assembly; there with the elohim [judges], he judges.
>
> —PSALM 82:1, CJB

> I have said, "You are gods, sons of the Most High, all of you.
>
> —PSALM 82:6

> Jesus answered them, "Is it not written in your law, 'I said, "You are gods"'? If He called them 'gods,' to whom the word of God came, and the Scripture cannot be broken..."
>
> —JOHN 10:34–35

Prophets are focused on the heart.

Prophets are concerned about the heart (motives). Outward shows don't impress them. They hate it when people honor God with their lips, but their hearts are far from Him. Prophets look for purity of heart. Prophets discern the heart. God looks at the heart.

Therefore, the Lord said: Because this people draw near with their mouths and honor Me with their lips, but have removed their hearts far from Me, and their fear toward Me is tradition by the precept of men...

—Isaiah 29:13

But the Lord said to Samuel, "Do not look on his appearance or on the height of his stature, because I have rejected him. For the Lord sees not as man sees. For man looks on the outward appearance, but the Lord looks on the heart."

—1 Samuel 16:7

Prophets are tenderhearted.

Although prophets can be tough and strong, they are also tenderhearted. David was tenderhearted when he was challenged by Nathan. *Tender* means showing gentleness and concern or sympathy. Synonyms include caring, kind, kindly, kindhearted, softhearted, tenderhearted, compassionate, sympathetic, warm, warmhearted, solicitous, fatherly, motherly, maternal, gentle, mild, benevolent, generous, giving, humane.

Because your heart was tender and you humbled yourself before God when you heard His words against this place and those who dwell here, and you have brought yourself low before Me and torn your clothes and wept before Me, I have heard you, declares the Lord.

—2 Chronicles 34:27

Prophets are God's representatives.

Prophets have a passion to see God represented correctly. They don't like it when God is misrepresented. They are fierce defenders of the truth and the truth of God. Don't misrepresent the Lord!

Prophets have godly jealousy.

Jealousy, in this case, really just shows you care about something passionately and don't want to see it destroyed. Prophets are protective.

They are protective of God's people and God's truth. They are protective of God's honor. Prophets will fight against anything that comes to kill, steal, and destroy. They will not just stand by and watch the enemy come in. They will raise their voices and do what is necessary.

> And he said, "I have been very zealous for the LORD, Lord of Hosts, for the children of Israel have forsaken Your covenant, thrown down Your altars, and killed Your prophets with the sword, and I alone am left, and they seek to take my life."
>
> —1 KINGS 19:10

God's name is jealous (Exod. 34:14).

Prophets are faithful (loyal).

Faithfulness and loyalty to God are important to prophets. They call back the backsliders. They challenge the church when there is unfaithfulness and disloyalty to God and His truth. Prophets preach commitment. They challenge anything and anyone that would draw the church away from God. They emphasize wholehearted loyalty and devotion to God in spite of changing times and what the world teaches.

Prophets are often considered too strict.

Some are considered too dogmatic. Prophets often ask themselves, "Am I being too strict? Am I being too dogmatic?" With prophets it is either obedience or disobedience. They have a standard, and that standard is obedience.

Prophets know the blessings of obedience, and the trouble with disobedience. Rebellious and disobedient people have a hard time with prophets.

Although prophets can sometimes seem strict, prophets are also merciful. They have the heart of God, which is both holiness and mercy.

If you are willing and obedient, you shall eat the good of the land; but if you refuse and rebel, you shall be devoured with the sword; for the mouth of the LORD has spoken it.

—ISAIAH 1:19–20

Prophets want us to experience the blessing of obedience.

Prophets are not mean or mean spirited. What prophets really desire is for us to be blessed and prosper through obedience. Prophets know that if we are willing and obedient we will eat the good of the land. Prophets want the best for the church and God's people. Prophets desire us to be above and not beneath, the head and not the tail, blessed coming in and blessed going out, lending and not borrowing, healthy, whole, peaceful, joyful, and wealthy.

If you are willing and obedient, you shall eat the good of the land…

—ISAIAH 1:19

Prophets have a high standard of holiness.

This can cause relationship issues with people who do not have high standards. Some people will consider prophets to have standards that are too high. Some will consider prophets too strict and too judgmental.

Pursue peace with all men, and the holiness without which no one will see the Lord…

—HEBREWS 12:14

Prophets raise and carry the standard.

A standard is a flag, a banner, a signal, an ensign. Standards draw, gather, and rally people to a cause. Banners can be seen from a distance. We need standard bearers. Standard bearers are those who gather and rally people for a godly cause. Prophets are standard bearers.

We no longer see our own banners; there is no longer any
prophet: neither is there among us any that knows. How long
shall this be?

—Psalm 74:9, jub

We will rejoice in your salvation, and in the name of our God
we will set up our banners; may the Lord fulfill all your
petitions.

—Psalm 20:5

Thou hast given a banner to them that fear thee, that it may
be displayed because of the truth. Selah.

—Psalm 60:4, kjv

Go through, go through the gates. Prepare the way of the
people; build up, build up the highway. Remove the stones;
lift up a standard over the peoples.

—Isaiah 62:10

Prophets want things done God's way.

God gives patterns and blueprints to prophets.

See that you make them according to their pattern which was
shown to you on the mountain.

—Exodus 25:40

Prophets are examples.

Prophets are to be examples to others: "My brothers, take the
prophets, who spoke in the name of the Lord, as an example of suffering and patience" (James 5:10).

Prophets are examples for how to endure suffering and how to
exercise patience, perseverance, and steadfastness.

Prophets are equalizers.

John came to fill the valleys and bring down the mountains.
Prophets help bring down the proud and lift up the humble. This
is equalization. This is leveling—equalization, demolishing, razing,
grading, leveling, tearing down.

> Every valley shall be filled and every mountain and hill shall
> be brought low; and the crooked shall be made straight and
> the rough ways shall be made smooth.
>
> —LUKE 3:5

Prophets understand the severity of God.

> Therefore consider the goodness and severity of God—
> severity toward those who fell, but goodness toward you, if
> you continue in His goodness. Otherwise, you also will be
> cut off.
>
> —ROMANS 11:22

Severity is God's strict justice. Prophets understand the severity
of God toward those with hard and impenitent hearts. We don't hear
much about severity today. *Severe* means "strict in discipline and judgment." God is merciful, but He is also at times severe.

Prophets must walk in balance between God's mercy and His
severity.

Prophets are awake.

Prophets are awake to the things of the Spirit, and they cannot
stand it when churches are asleep. They are awake to what God is
doing. When others are sleeping, the prophet is awake. Prophets
wonder why others are sleeping. Prophets can't sleep like everyone
else. God does not let them sleep. They can't slumber. Prophets cry,
"Wake up!"

> Therefore He says: "Awake, you who sleep, arise from the
> dead, and Christ will give you light."
>
> —EPHESIANS 5:14

> Awake, awake! Put on your strength, O Zion; put on your
> beautiful garments, O Jerusalem, the holy city. For the uncir-
> cumcised and the unclean will no longer enter you.
>
> —ISAIAH 52:1

Prophets are concerned about the glory of God.

God's glory is important to prophets. They want God to be glorified in all things, and they will oppose anything or anyone who tries to take away from His glory. God's glory is His honor, power, fame, holiness, majesty, and authority. Prophets are promoters and defenders of the glory of God. They will pull down anything that exalts itself and tries to take the glory of God.

> If anyone speaks, let him speak as the oracles of God. If anyone serves, let him serve with the strength that God supplies, so that God in all things may be glorified through Jesus Christ, to whom be praise and dominion forever and ever. Amen.
>
> —1 PETER 4:11

Prophets have sharp discernment (or radar).

This is a strong point in prophets. They discern. This is sometimes hard to handle because they are sensitive to the spirit realm.

> *Discernment* in the Greek language means judicial estimation, discern, disputation. It comes from a word meaning to separate thoroughly, withdraw, oppose, discriminate, decide, hesitate, contend, make to differ, doubt, judge, be partial, stagger, and waver…
>
> When the discerner is confronted with something that appears good on the outside, but isn't, it becomes a stumbling block to his spirit. His flesh sees good signs, but his spirit is disputing, opposing, hesitating, contending, differing, doubting, staggering, and wavering against the outward appearance. Discernment is an internal war as one grapples to line up what they perceive, with Who God is, and what is being offered.[2]

> But solid food belongs to those who are mature, for those who through practice have powers of discernment that are trained to distinguish good from evil.
>
> —HEBREWS 5:14

Prophets know when it's time to move in a new direction.

Prophets hate going around in circles. They know when it's time to stop circling the mountain.

> You have circled this mountain long enough. Now turn north.
>
> —DEUTERONOMY 2:3

Prophets see the measure.

Ezekiel saw the measuring rod of the house of the Lord. He also saw the measure of the river (depth of the waters—ankle high, knee high, shoulder high). *Measure* means "to ascertain the dimensions, quantity, or capacity of." Prophets can see the depth of holiness, prayer, worship, revelation, love, outreach, and the like. Measuring helps us know where we are, and in what areas we need to increase.

> The man said to me, "Son of man, look with your eyes, and hear with your ears, and set your heart on all that I shall show you. For you have been brought here to show it to you. Declare all that you see to the house of Israel."
>
> There was a wall all around the outside of the temple. In the man's hand was a measuring reed of six cubits long, each being a cubit and a handbreadth. So he measured the width of the building, one reed. And the height, one reed.
>
> —EZEKIEL 40:4–5

> Again he measured a thousand and brought me through the water. The water reached the knees. Again he measured a thousand and brought me through the water. The water reached the loins. Afterward he measured a thousand. And it

was a river that I could not pass over, for the water had risen,
enough water to swim in, a river that could not be passed over.

—EZEKIEL 47:4–5

Prophets are good evangelists.

Everyone should evangelize, including prophets. Prophets are
good at evangelizing because they have discernment and sensitivity to
the conditions of people, including the lost. Prophets bring conviction
when they minister, and conviction is a part of successful evangelism.

Prophetic churches will also have many salvations because of a
strong presence of God and the convicting power of the Holy Spirit.
Prophets will also carry the burden of the Lord for the lost.

> But if all prophesy [giving inspired testimony and inter-
> preting the divine will and purpose] and an unbeliever or
> untaught outsider comes in, he is told of his sin and reproved
> and convicted and convinced by all, and his defects and needs
> are examined (estimated, determined) and he is called to
> account by all.
>
> —1 CORINTHIANS 14:24, AMP

Sometimes nonbelievers respond to prophets better than believers.

Someone just pointed this out to me. The city of Nineveh repented
at the preaching of Jonah. Jesus said that Sodom would have repented
at His works. Elijah was sent to a Gentile widow. Elisha healed a
Gentile leper.

> He also said, "Truly, I say to you, no prophet is accepted
> in his own country. But I tell you truthfully, many widows
> were in Israel in the days of Elijah, when the heavens were
> closed for three years and six months, when great famine was
> throughout all the land. Yet to none of them was Elijah sent
> except to Zarephath, a city of Sidon, to a woman who was a
> widow.
>
> —LUKE 4:24–26

And you, Capernaum, who is exalted toward heaven, will be brought down to Hades. For if the mighty works which have been done in you had been done in Sodom, it would have remained until this day.

—MATTHEW 11:23

Prophets are good deliverance ministers.

Prophets generally operate with the gifts of discerning of spirits and the word of knowledge, which are invaluable when ministering deliverance. Prophets can "hit the nail on the head" when it comes to demons and casting them out. Their spiritual insight and sensitivity help greatly when ministering deliverance.

I have also seen many people delivered through the prophetic word.

He sent His word and healed them and delivered them from their destruction.

—PSALM 107:20

Prophets are cutting edge.

Prophets are usually the first ones to embrace change and the new thing God is doing. They understand and embrace new moves of God. If you want to be a part of cutting-edge people of the Spirit, then get around prophets. Prophets hate stagnation and old wine. Prophets love new wine and new wineskins.

Prophets release freshness.

Prophets fear the Lord.

Prophets understand and promote the fear of the Lord. They stand up when people lose the fear of the Lord. Prophets promote reverence for God and the things of the Spirit. To a prophet, there cannot be true success and blessing without the fear of the Lord.

Sanctify the LORD of Hosts Himself, and let Him be your fear, and let Him be your dread.

—ISAIAH 8:13

Prophets bring reverence for God (trembling).

Many have lost reverence for God. What has happened to trembling? Prophets stand up when reverence is lost.

> Serve the LORD with fear,; tremble with trepidation!
>
> —PSALM 2:11

> Do you not fear and reverence Me? says the Lord. Do you not tremble before Me? I placed the sand for the boundary of the sea, a perpetual barrier beyond which it cannot pass and by an everlasting ordinance beyond which it cannot go? And though the waves of the sea toss and shake themselves, yet they cannot prevail [against the feeble grains of sand which God has ordained by nature to be sufficient for His purpose]; though [the billows] roar, yet they cannot pass over that [barrier]. [Is not such a God to be reverently feared and worshiped?]
>
> —JEREMIAH 5:22, AMP

> Therefore, my beloved, as you have always obeyed, not only in my presence, but so much more in my absence, work out your own salvation with fear and trembling.
>
> —PHILIPPIANS 2:12

Prophets expose idolatry.

Idolatry is more than worshipping images. Idolatry is anything that replaces God. Worship and exaltation of men, ministry, power, possessions, groups, and fame is nothing but idolatry. Covetousness is called idolatry. Prophets are fierce opponents of idols. Prophets stand against idolatry creeping into the church.

> You shall have no other gods before Me.
>
> —EXODUS 20:3

> Little children, keep yourselves from idols.
>
> —1 JOHN 5:21

Therefore put to death the parts of your earthly nature: sexual immorality, uncleanness, inordinate affection, evil desire, and covetousness, which is idolatry.

—COLOSSIANS 3:5

Prophets expose reprobates (continual rejection of God).

A reprobate is a morally unprincipled person; shameless; a depraved, unprincipled, or wicked person; rejected by God and without hope of salvation. Continual rejection of God and His Spirit is dangerous and wicked. (See Acts 7:51.)

And since they did not see fit to acknowledge God, God gave them over to a debased mind, to do those things which are not proper.

—ROMANS 1:28

Examine yourselves, whether ye be in the faith; prove your own selves. Know ye not your own selves, how that Jesus Christ is in you, except ye be reprobates?

—2 CORINTHIANS 13:5, KJV

Now as Jannes and Jambres resisted Moses, so these also resist the truth, men of corrupt minds and worthless concerning the faith.

—2 TIMOTHY 3:8

They profess that they know God; but in works they deny him, being abominable, and disobedient, and unto every good work reprobate.

—TITUS 1:16, KJV

Prophets expose foxes (craftiness).

A fox is a crafty, sly, or clever person. This craftiness can also be personified in weasels, which is a person regarded as sneaky or treacherous.

Catch the foxes for us, the little foxes that spoil the vineyards, for our vineyards are in blossom.

—SONG OF SONGS 2:15

O Israel, your prophets are like the foxes in the ruins.

—EZEKIEL 13:4

He said to them, "Go and tell that fox, 'Look, I cast out demons. And I perform healings today and tomorrow, and on the third day I shall be perfected.'"

—LUKE 13:32

He perceived their craftiness and said to them, "Why do you test Me?"

—LUKE 20:23

Prophets expose seducers and seducing spirits.

Seduce means "to attract or lead (someone) away from proper behavior or thinking; to induce (someone) to engage in sexual activity, as by flirting or persuasion; to entice into a different state or position."

Now the Spirit clearly says that in the last times some will depart from the faith and pay attention to seducing spirits and doctrines of devils.

—1 TIMOTHY 4:1

But evil men and seducers will grow worse and worse, deceiving and being deceived.

—2 TIMOTHY 3:13

I have written these things to you concerning those who deceive you.

—1 JOHN 2:26

But I have a few things against you: You permit that woman Jezebel, who calls herself a prophetess, to teach and seduce My servants to commit sexual immorality and eat food sacrificed to idols.

—REVELATION 2:20

Prophets expose the spirit of mammon.

Mammon is greed, covetousness, and the love of money. Jesus exposed it among the leaders in Israel. You cannot serve God and mammon. False prophets are controlled by mammon. True prophets expose mammon.

> No man can serve two masters: for either he will hate the one, and love the other; or else he will hold to the one, and despise the other. Ye cannot serve God and mammon.
> —MATTHEW 6:24, KJV

> For the love of money is the root of all evil. While coveting after money, some have strayed from the faith and pierced themselves through with many sorrows.
> —1 TIMOTHY 6:10

Prophets expose hidden things.

Prophets will see hidden pride, hidden ambition, hidden lust, hidden witchcraft, hidden wickedness, hidden agendas, and hidden lies.

> Woe to those who deeply hide their counsel from the LORD and whose works are done in the dark, and they say, "Who sees us?" and "Who knows us?"
> —ISAIAH 29:15

> How the things of Esau have been ransacked! How his hidden treasures hunted out!
> —OBADIAH 1:6

Prophets expose hypocrisy.

Notice in Matthew 6:2–16, 23:3–29, and other places throughout Matthew how much Jesus (the Prophet like unto Moses) spoke about hypocrisy. Hypocrisy is the practice of claiming to have moral standards or beliefs to which one's own behavior does not conform; pretense.

> You hypocrites, Isaiah well prophesied of you.
> —MATTHEW 15:7

And in the morning, "It will be foul weather today, for the sky is red and overcast." O you hypocrites, you can discern the face of the sky, but you cannot discern the signs of the times.

—MATTHEW 16:3

But Jesus perceived their wickedness and said, "Why test Me, you hypocrites?"

—MATTHEW 22:18

Therefore, whatever they tell you to observe, that observe and do, but do not do their works. For they speak, but do nothing.

—MATTHEW 23:3

Woe to you, scribes and Pharisees, hypocrites! You shut the kingdom of heaven against men. For you neither enter yourselves, nor allow those who are entering to go in.

—MATTHEW 23:13

And will cut him in pieces and appoint him his portion with the hypocrites, where there shall be weeping and gnashing of teeth.

—MATTHEW 24:51

Prophets want people to experience God.

Jacob called the name of the place Peniel, saying, "I have seen God face to face, and my life has been preserved."

—GENESIS 32:30

Dreams, visions, glory, weeping, visitations at night, under the power for long periods of time, angels—these are what prophets want others to experience in the presence of God.

Prophets want to see something done.

When there is a need, a problem, a situation, or an error, prophets don't just want to talk about it. They want action! They sometimes get into trouble because they press for action and change. They hate when nothing is done and people just cover up and delay.

Prophets are focused and like praying the plans and purposes of God.

Prophets don't want to just pray about anything and everything. Prophets want to "zero in" on what God wants to do. They want to hit the "bull's-eye." Prophets are focused on the will of God in a situation. If you want to hit the target, ask a prophet to pray.

Prophets look for rivers.

Prophets like the flow of the Spirit. The flow of the Spirit is likened unto a river. The river of God is important to prophets. They like river churches and river believers. They want to know where God's power is flowing.

Prophets don't like when the flow of the Spirit is blocked. Prophets work to remove the obstacles that block the river. They like to be in services where there is a strong flow of the Spirit. Prophets want to see the river of God flow in their regions and territories.

> There is a river whose streams make glad the city of God, the holy dwelling place of the Most High.
>
> —PSALM 46:4

> He who believes in Me, as the Scripture has said, out of his heart shall flow rivers of living water.
>
> —JOHN 7:38

Prophets look for rivers, currents, flow, living water, river churches, spiritual dams.

Prophets dig wells.

Prophets will dig wells where there is no water. They don't like when the things of the Spirit are plugged and stopped up. They are like Isaac, who redug the wells the Philistines had stopped up. They will re-dig the wells that have been stopped up in a region by sin, apathy, and compromise. Prophets dig new wells and open old wells. Prophets will get the water flowing.

If you want the wells unstopped and the water released, get a prophet.

> Isaac dug again the wells of water, which they had dug in the days of Abraham his father, for the Philistines had stopped them up after the death of Abraham. He called their names after the names his father had called them.
>
> —GENESIS 26:18

Prophets build the waste places.

Like Nehemiah, prophets rebuild. They build the old waste places. They raise up the former desolations. They repair the waste cities. Prophets repair, rebuild, restore.

> They shall build the old ruins; they shall raise up the former desolations, and they shall repair the waste cities, the desolations of many generations.
>
> —ISAIAH 61:4

Prophets are repairers of the breach and restorers of paths to dwell in.

Prophets deal with ruins, broken walls, lost paths, and fallen foundations in the lives of people. Prophets are all about rebuilding, repairing, and restoring the lives of the broken.

> Those from among you shall rebuild the old waste places; you shall raise up the foundations of many generations; and you shall be called, the Repairer of the Breach, the Restorer of Paths in which to Dwell.
>
> —ISAIAH 58:12

Prophets stand in the breach.

This is intercession. This is pleading on the behalf of people. This is standing in the gap. This is asking for mercy.

> Therefore He said that He would destroy them, had not Moses, His chosen one, stood before Him to intercede, to turn away His wrath from destroying them.
>
> —PSALM 106:23

> I sought for a man among them who would build up the hedge and stand in the gap before Me for the land so that I would not destroy it, but I found no one.
>
> —EZEKIEL 22:30

Prophets repair altars.

An altar is a place of sacrifice, consecration, worship, prayer, glory, and manifestation.

> Elijah said to all the people, "Come near to me." And all the people came near to him. And he repaired the altar of the LORD that was broken down.
>
> —1 KINGS 18:30

> Then I will go to the altar of God, to the God of my joyful gladness; with the harp I will give thanks to You, O God, my God.
>
> —PSALM 43:4

Prophets want to see deliverance and restoration.

> But this is a people robbed and despoiled; they are all snared in holes, and they are hidden in prison houses; they are for a prey, and no one delivers, for a spoil, and no one says, "Restore them."
>
> —ISAIAH 42:22

Prophets turn hearts (reconciliation).

Prophets deal with heart issues. The prophet's ministry turns the heart, and brings reconciliation between those who have been separated.

> And he shall turn and reconcile the hearts of the [estranged] fathers to the [ungodly] children, and the hearts of the

[rebellious] children to [the piety of] their fathers [a reconciliation produced by repentance of the ungodly], lest I come
and smite the land with a curse and a ban of utter destruction.
—MALACHI 4:6, AMP

Prophets have intimacy with God.

Intimacy is a strength of a prophet. The prophet knows how to
withdraw and get with God. Intimacy is about a close, familiar, and
usually affectionate or loving personal relationship with another
person or group. Prophets love being alone with God. Prophets love
ministering to the Lord (worshipping).

Prophets cultivate intimacy with the Father and hear His voice.
Fasting, prayer, and ministering to the Lord are all part of how
prophets draw near to God.

> My beloved speaks and says to me: "Rise up, my love, my fair
> one, and come away."
> —SONG OF SONGS 2:10

> As they worshipped the Lord and fasted, the Holy Spirit said,
> "Set apart for Me Barnabas and Saul for the work to which I
> have called them."
> —ACTS 13:2

Prophets are covenant messengers.

The prophets were sent by the king to call Israel back to covenant. Prophets are concerned about covenant. The church is the
New Testament covenant community. Broken covenant (fellowship)
will grieve prophets. Prophets demand that we live up to our covenant obligations.

> The earth also is defiled by its inhabitants because they have
> transgressed the laws, violated the ordinances, broken the
> everlasting covenant.
> —ISAIAH 24:5

Now may the God of peace, who through the blood of the eternal covenant brought again from the dead our Lord Jesus, the Great Shepherd of the sheep…

—Hebrews 13:20

Prophets look for fruit.

Jesus came to Israel looking for fruit. Jesus cursed the fig tree because it had no fruit. Israel was religious but fruitless. Fruit is important to God and to the prophet. Prophets hate barrenness. Prophets need more than talk, sermons, prayers, and religious activity. Prophets look for fruit. Prophets are grieved at fruitlessness.

Everything that does not bear fruit is cut down.

Therefore, bear fruit worthy of repentance.

—Matthew 3:8

When He saw a fig tree by the road, He went to it but found nothing on it except leaves. He said to it, "Let no fruit ever grow on you again." Immediately the fig tree withered away.

—Matthew 21:19

So he said to the vinedresser of his vineyard, "Now these three years I have come looking for fruit on this fig tree, and I find none. Cut it down. Why should it deplete the soil?"

—Luke 13:7

Prophets look for works.

The prophet says, "Faith without works is dead." Prophets hate the claim to faith without corresponding actions. I like the Amplified Version of James 2:17, "So also faith, if it does not have works (deeds and actions of obedience to back it up), by itself is destitute of power (inoperative, dead)."

So faith by itself, if it has no works, is dead.

—James 2:17

Prophets look at deeds.

Prophets don't go by what people say but what they do (their deeds). A deed is something that is carried out; an act or action. They either produce evil deeds or righteous deeds.

> Not everyone who says to Me, "Lord, Lord," shall enter the kingdom of heaven, but he who does the will of My Father who is in heaven.
> —MATTHEW 7:21

> For everyone who does evil hates the light and does not come to the light, lest his deeds should be exposed. But he who does the truth comes to the light, that it may be revealed that his deeds have been done in God.
> —JOHN 3:20–21

> "You are doing the works of your father." Then they said to Him, "We were not born of sexual immorality. We have one Father: God."
> —JOHN 8:41

> My little children, let us love not in word and speech, but in action and truth.
> —1 JOHN 3:18

> And blasphemed the God of heaven because of their pains and their sores, and did not repent of their deeds.
> —REVELATION 16:11

Prophets look for sincerity.

Sincere means "not feigned or affected; genuine; being without hypocrisy or pretense; true; pure; unadulterated."

> Therefore let us keep the feast, not with old yeast, nor with the yeast of malice and wickedness, but with the unleavened bread of sincerity and truth.
> —1 CORINTHIANS 5:8

For we are not as many, which corrupt the word of God: but as of sincerity, but as of God, in the sight of God speak we in Christ.

—2 Corinthians 2:17, kjv

In all things shewing thyself a pattern of good works: in doctrine shewing uncorruptness, gravity, sincerity,

—Titus 2:7, kjv

Prophets look for tears (weeping).

Tears (weeping) is a sign of a contrite spirit. Prophets look for real repentance and tears when there is a need to return to the Lord.

The sacrifices of God are a broken spirit; a broken and a contrite heart, O God, You will not despise.

—Psalm 51:17

Those who sow in tears shall reap in joy.

—Psalm 126:5

Yet even now, declares the Lord, return to Me with all your heart, and with fasting and with weeping and with mourning.

—Joel 2:12

Prophets don't judge by outward appearance.

Prophets look at what is inside. They are not fooled by the outward appearance.

Woe to you, scribes and Pharisees, hypocrites! You are like whitewashed tombs, which indeed appear beautiful outwardly, but inside are full of dead men's bones and of all uncleanness.

—Matthew 23:27

Prophets hunger and thirst for righteousness.

One of the prime motivations of prophets is a desire to do and see what is right. Prophets hate unrighteousness. Prophets have a strong desire to see things done and set right. This is what satisfies the prophet.

Blessed are those who hunger and thirst for righteousness, for
they shall be filled.

—MATTHEW 5:6

Great blessings belong to those who want to do right more
than anything else. God will fully satisfy them.

—MATTHEW 5:6, ERV

Prophets can identify children of the devil.

In other words, prophets can identify people who are being used
and controlled by the devil to bring harm and destruction. Jesus identified people this way. Paul identified Elymas the sorcerer this way.
Prophets can identify the enemies of God and His kingdom.

You are of your father the devil, and you want to do the
desires of your father. He was a murderer from the beginning,
and does not stand in the truth, because there is no truth in
him. When he lies, he speaks from his own nature, for he is a
liar and the father of lies.

—JOHN 8:44

You son of the devil, enemy of all righteousness, full of deceit
and of all fraud, will you not cease perverting the right ways
of the Lord?

—ACTS 13:10

Prophets cannot tolerate evil.

Tolerate means "to allow the existence, presence, practice, or act
of without prohibition or hindrance; permit." Prophets will speak up
against evil.

Whoever privately slanders his neighbor, him I will destroy;
whoever has a haughty look and a proud heart I will not
endure.

—PSALM 101:5

For [you seem readily to endure it] if a man comes and
preaches another Jesus than the One we preached, or if you
receive a different spirit from the [Spirit] you [once] received

or a different gospel from the one you [then] received and welcomed; you tolerate [all that] well enough!

—2 CORINTHIANS 11:4, AMP

But I have this against you: that you tolerate the woman Jezebel, who calls herself a prophetess [claiming to be inspired], and who is teaching and leading astray my servants and beguiling them into practicing sexual vice and eating food sacrificed to idols.

—REVELATION 2:20, AMP

Prophets battle (contend) against the wicked.

Those who abandon Instruction praise the wicked, but those who follow Instruction battle them.

—PROVERBS 28:4, CEB

Those who abandon God's teachings praise wicked people, but those who follow God's teachings oppose wicked people.

—PROVERBS 28:4, GW

I confronted the officials and asked, "Why is the house of God forsaken?" So I gathered them and stationed them at their posts.

—NEHEMIAH 13:11

You shall seek them and shall not find them, even those who contended with you. Those who war against you shall be as nothing, as a thing of nonexistence.

—ISAIAH 41:12

Prophets don't whitewash evil.

Whitewash is a mixture of lime and water, often with whiting, size, or glue added, that is used to whiten walls, fences, or other structures. It means to conceal or gloss over (wrongdoing, for example).

When the wall has collapsed, people will ask you, "Where is the whitewash you coated it with?"

—EZEKIEL 13:12, NET

Prophets speak when the wicked prosper.

Prophets speak and pray when the wicked prosper. They stand up when it seems as if the wicked are prospering and the righteous are struggling. Prophets remind us that it will not go well with the wicked and the righteous should not fret.

> Rest in the Lord, and wait patiently for Him; do not fret because of those who prosper in their way, because of those who make wicked schemes.
>
> —PSALM 37:7

> Hope in the LORD, and keep His way, and He will exalt you to inherit the land; when the wicked are cut off, you will see it. I have seen the wicked in great power, and spreading himself like a luxuriant tree. Yet he passed away, and he was not; I sought him, but he could not be found.
>
> —PSALM 37:34–36

> For I was envious at the boastful; I saw the prosperity of the wicked.
>
> —PSALM 73:3

> Observe, these are the wicked, always at ease; they increase in riches.
>
> —PSALM 73:12

Prophets take a stand against immorality.

Sexual sin, greed, wasteful living, impurity, and other immoralities prophets will not stand for.

> Shun immorality and all sexual looseness [flee from impurity in thought, word, or deed]. Any other sin which a man commits is one outside the body, but he who commits sexual immorality sins against his own body.
>
> —1 CORINTHIANS 6:18, AMP

> But immorality (sexual vice) and all impurity [of lustful, rich, wasteful living] or greediness must not even be named among

you, as is fitting and proper among saints (God's consecrated people).

—EPHESIANS 5:3, AMP

Let us live and conduct ourselves honorably and becomingly as in the [open light of] day, not in reveling (carousing) and drunkenness, not in immorality and debauchery (sensuality and licentiousness), not in quarreling and jealousy.

—ROMANS 13:13, AMP

Prophets don't walk and agree with just anyone.

Prophets don't agree with everything. Agree means "to accept or support a policy or program."

Do two people walk together, if they have not agreed?

—AMOS 3:3

What agreement has the temple of God with idols? For you are the temple of the living God. As God has said: "I will live in them and walk in them. I will be their God, and they shall be My people."

—2 CORINTHIANS 6:16

Prophets understand God ordained relationships.

Relationships are very important to prophets. Relationships are important to destiny. God ordained relationships are a part of fulfilling your destiny and purpose.

+ Husband-wife relationships
+ Ministry relationships
+ Father-son relationships
+ Covenant relationships

The prophet asks, "Are you connected to the right people?"

What therefore God has joined together, let not man put asunder.

—MARK 10:9

As they worshipped the Lord and fasted, the Holy Spirit said, "Set apart for Me Barnabas and Saul for the work to which I have called them."

—ACTS 13:2

Prophets let you know when you are connected to the wrong people.

Eliezer prophesied to Jehoshaphat concerning his connection with the wicked king Amaziah. This connection caused his works to fail. People who want to be in relationships that are not ordained of God may resent this. Prophets will let you know when you are bound by bad soul ties or ungodly connections.

And Eliezer son of Dodavahu from Mareshah prophesied against Jehoshaphat saying, "Because you have joined with Ahaziah, the LORD will tear down your works." So the ships were wrecked, so that they were not able to journey to Tarshish.

—2 CHRONICLES 20:37

Do not be so deceived and misled! Evil companionships (communion, associations) corrupt and deprave good manners and morals and character.

—1 CORINTHIANS 15:33, AMP

Prophets are iconoclasts (Nehushtan).

An iconoclast is a breaker of idols. The children of Israel began to worship the brazen serpent that God instructed Moses to raise in the wilderness. The brazen serpent became an idol. It was later smashed. Sometimes old moves of God have become idols. The prophet will smash these idols.

An iconoclast is a person who attacks cherished beliefs, traditional institutions, and the like, as being based on error or superstition. These iconoclast characteristics apply to apostles as well.

He removed the high places, and brake the images, and cut down the groves, and brake in pieces the brasen serpent that

Moses had made: for unto those days the children of Israel did burn incense to it: and *he called it Nehushtan.*
—2 KINGS 18:4, KJV, EMPHASIS ADDED

Prophets are insiders who think like outsiders.

God uses prophets to keep the church on course. Sometimes it takes a person on the outside to see clearly and press for change. I call the prophet an insider who sees like an outsider. The prophet sometimes feels like an outsider, although the prophet is a member of the faith community. Insiders tend to be nearsighted and sometimes cannot see the forest for the trees. I want to emphasize that the prophet is a member of the church.

Outsiders can be critical of what is happening because they see things differently. Outsiders can be more objective. Sometimes insiders reject all critique from outsiders, but often the outsider is right. The outsider has nothing to lose. The outsider is not invested like the insider.

Prophets think outside the box.

This is a metaphor that means to think differently, unconventionally, or from a new perspective. Prophets cannot fit in the box. Prophets stretch us. Prophets help us break limitations. They are visionaries. They help us move out of ruts and routine. They not only think outside the box, but they also help us break out of the box.

Religion and tradition can become a box. Limitations, thinking, mind-sets, barriers, and so on are other boxes.

Prophets are problem solvers.

When Pharaoh had a problem (a dream), he called Joseph. When King Nebuchadnezzar had a problem (a dream), he called Daniel. Daniel was described as a man who solved "knotty problems."

If you have a problem, get with a prophet. Prophets have solutions.

Because an excellent spirit, knowledge, and understanding to interpret dreams, clarify riddles, and solve knotty problems

were found in this same Daniel, whom the king named
Belteshazzar. Now let Daniel be called, and he will show the
interpretation.

—DANIEL 5:12, AMP

Prophets are people of vision.

Prophets have to have vision. They cannot live aimless lives. They
want to know what the vision is. They want to know where we are
going. They want to know where the church is going. They ask, "What
does the future hold?"

Where there is no vision, the people perish; but happy is he
who keeps the teaching.

—PROVERBS 29:18

And the LORD answered me: Write the vision, and make it
plain on tablets, that he who reads it may run.

—HABAKKUK 2:2

The prophet is a spark plug.

A spark plug is one who gives life or energy to an endeavor.
Prophets are catalysts. Synonyms for *catalyst* include stimulus, stimulation, spark, spark plug, spur, incitement, impetus.

Prophets help get things moving. Prophets like to get things
moving. They hate when things are stagnant and not moving. They
are like a spark that ignites. Their words ignite. Their prayers ignite.
Their songs ignite.

Prophets don't settle for less.

Prophets know there is more to come.

Prophets know there is more to do.

Prophets know there is more to experience.

Prophets know there is more to know.

Prophets know there is more to believe.

Prophets know there is more to happen.

Prophets know there is more to see.

Prophets know there is more to hear.

> Now to Him who is able to do exceedingly abundantly
> beyond all that we ask or imagine, according to the power
> that works in us.
> —Ephesians 3:20

Prophets are contenders (fighters).

Contend means struggle to surmount (a difficulty or danger). To contend means to fight or battle. Contenders are overcomers. Contenders fight for truth. Contenders fight for justice. Prophets always seem to be fighting something. Prophets can sometimes think, "Am I the only one fighting this?" That is the nature of a prophet: they are fighters.

> Beloved, while I diligently tried to write to you of the salvation we have in common, I found it necessary to write and appeal to you to contend for the faith which was once delivered to the saints.
> —Jude 1:3

> Those who forsake instruction praise the wicked, but such as keep instruction contend with them.
> Proverbs 28:4

Prophets are Zadoks.

Zadoks were the faithful priests who did not go astray like other Levites. God commended them for their faithfulness and obedience. Faithfulness to God is a priority with prophets. Zadok was also a seer.

> The king also said to Zadok the priest, "Are you not a seer? Return to the city in peace with your two sons, your son Ahimaaz and Jonathan the son of Abiathar."
> —2 Samuel 15:27

> But the Levitical priests, the sons of Zadok, who kept the charge of My sanctuary when the sons of Israel went astray from Me, they shall come near to Me to minister to Me, and

they shall stand before Me to offer to Me the fat and the blood, says the Lord GOD.

—EZEKIEL 44:15

It shall be for the priests who are sanctified of the sons of Zadok, who have kept My charge, who did not go astray when the sons of Israel went astray as the Levites went astray.

—EZEKIEL 48:11

Prophets know their people.

Prophets know the people they are assigned to. They know their good points, and they know their bad points. Jesus knew the Jews and dealt with them strongly. Prophets are honest. Prophets tell their people the truth.

> One of them, a prophet of their own, said, "The Cretans are always liars, evil beasts, and idle gluttons!" This witness is true. So rebuke them sharply that they may be sound in the faith.
>
> —TITUS 1:12–13

Prophets speak to the remnant.

Prophets spoke to the remnant in Israel. There was always a true Israel within Israel. They were promised salvation, deliverance, and restoration. The remnant are the faithful. Prophets bless and encourage the remnant.

> Still, I have preserved seven thousand men in Israel for Myself, all of whose knees have not bowed to Baal and whose mouths have not kissed him.
>
> —1 KINGS 19:18

> For from Jerusalem shall go out a remnant, and those who escape out of Mount Zion. The zeal of the LORD of Hosts shall do this.
>
> —ISAIAH 37:32

> Then the dragon was angry with the woman, and he went to wage war with the remnant of her offspring, who keep

the commandments of God and have the testimony of Jesus
Christ.

—REVELATION 12:17

Prophets challenge those who claim to be God's people.

Prophets were sent to challenge those who claimed to be God's
people. Israel claimed it in name but denied it in action. Hosea named
one of his children Loammi which meant "ye are not my people."
Prophets are concerned about those who are supposed to be God's
people. A common phrase throughout Scripture is "and ye shall be my
people, and I will be your God."

Prophets want your action to line up with your claim.

Then the LORD said: "Call his name Lo-Ammi, for you are
not My people, and I am not your God."

—HOSEA 1:9

Prophets plead.

Plead means to present and argue for (a position), especially in
court or in another public context. Prophets plead for those who have
no advocate. They plead for those who have no voice. They plead in
prayer. They plead with their voices.

Prophets also plead for the righteous.

Open thy mouth, judge righteously, and plead the cause of
the poor and needy.

—PROVERBS 31:9

Learn to do good; seek justice, relieve the oppressed; judge
the fatherless, plead for the widow.

—ISAIAH 1:17

No one calls for justice, nor does anyone plead for truth. They
trust in vanity and speak lies; they conceive mischief and
bring forth iniquity.

—ISAIAH 59:4

Prophets are servants.

Prophets are God's servants, and they also serve man. The term *servant* implies subservience and humility. The Hebrew term is *ebed*, which also has the connotation of an official or an officer, especially an officer of a royal court. The greatest in the kingdom is the servant.

Prophets serve in an official capacity.

> We have not listened to Your servants the prophets, who spoke in Your name.
>
> —DANIEL 9:6

> Surely the Lord GOD does nothing without revealing His purpose to His servants the prophets.
>
> —AMOS 3:7

Prophets are the burning ones.

In Isaiah 6:1–8 *seraphim* is the word Isaiah used to describe fiery beings that fly around God's throne singing, "Holy, holy, holy." It translates in Hebrew to literally "burning ones." There is a new breed of prophets arising in this season who are sent out by the throne of heaven to deliver the word of the Lord. These prophets are the burning ones for this age. They will speak as the prophets of old, burning with a fire that will not be contained. The word of the Lord in their hearts is like a burning fire. They will ignite the world with this word.

> But if I say, "I will not make mention of Him nor speak any more in His name," then His word was in my heart as a burning fire shut up in my bones; and I was weary of forbearing it, and I could not endure it.
>
> —JEREMIAH 20:9

Prophets preach the reality not the shadow.

The Law was a shadow, but Christ is the reality. The shadows (types and symbols) are fulfilled in Christ. Prophets help us get away from the shadows so we can experience the fulfillment in Christ. Prophets deal with spiritual realities, not shadows and types such as

Passover, Pentecost, Day of Atonement, dietary laws, circumcision, sabbaths, and the like.

Prophets have ears to hear.

If anyone has ears to hear what the Lord is saying to the church, it should be the prophets. Where were the prophets in the seven churches of Asia (Rev. 1–3)? The Lord sent a word to the seven churches and was speaking to those who had ears to hear. The Lord sends His word to churches and looks for those who have ears to hear.

> He who has an ear, let him hear what the Spirit says to the churches. To him who overcomes I will give permission to eat of the tree of life, which is in the midst of the Paradise of God.
>
> —REVELATION 2:7

Prophets hear the still, small voice.

Sometimes the Lord is not in the wind, the earthquake, or in the fire, but in the still small voice. The prophet can hear the still small voice in the midst of the wind, the earthquake, and the fire. The prophet does not get caught up in the dramatic, but can hear the still, small voice. The prophet sometimes has to get quiet to hear this voice, "What is God saying that I can hear only when I quiet down and listen to what He is saying deep within?"

Get quiet, prophets, and let God speak to you in the still, small voice.

> He said, "Go and stand on the mountain before the LORD." And, behold, the LORD passed by, and a great and strong wind split the mountains and broke in pieces the rocks before the LORD, but the LORD was not in the wind. And after the wind, an earthquake came, but the LORD was not in the earthquake. And after the earthquake, a fire came, but the LORD was not in the fire, and after the fire, a still, small voice. When Elijah heard it, he wrapped his face in his cloak and went out and

stood in the entrance to the cave. And a voice came to him and said, "Why are you here, Elijah?"

—1 Kings 19:11–13

Prophets remind us that power (strength) belongs to God.

Strength comes from God. God is the source of power and strength. Prophets encourage us to draw from God's strength.

God says there is one thing you can really depend on, and I believe it: "Strength comes from God!"

—Psalm 62:11, erv

God has spoken once, twice have I heard this: that power belongs to God.

—Psalm 62:11

O God, You are awesome from Your sanctuaries; the God of Israel is He who gives strength and power to people. Blessed be God!

—Psalm 68:35

Do not fear, for I am with you; do not be dismayed, for I am your God. I will strengthen you, I will help you, yes, I will uphold you with My righteous right hand.

—Isaiah 41:10

Prophets remind us, "It's by the Spirit."

No program can replace the power of the Spirit. Entertainment does not replace the power of the Spirit. Prophets will cry out whenever churches moves away from the power of the Spirit.

And he said to me: "This is the word of the Lord to Zerubbabel, saying: Not by might nor by power, but by My Spirit, says the Lord of Hosts.

—Zechariah 4:6

3

WHAT MOVES THE HEART OF A PROPHET?

God gave Solomon wisdom and great depth of understanding
as well as compassion, as vast as the sand on the seashore.

—1 Kings 4:29

IN PROPHETS WE see many sides to God's heart—compassion, hatred of sin and unrighteousness, holiness, grief, encouragement, power, joy, zeal, and so on. The prophet carries within them the heart of the Father. They feel what the Father feels at different times. This can be a difficult thing for prophets to learn to handle. The prophet can feel as if they are on an emotional roller coaster.

Don't fret, prophet, and don't be confused. You are special. You carry within your heart the heartbeat of God.

David was a man after God's own heart.

> The LORD has sought for Himself a man after His own heart and the LORD has commanded him to be prince over His people.
>
> —1 Samuel 13:14

Prophets have big hearts. This chapter reveals how deep and wide the prophet's heart is. God gives prophets His heart. Prophets are in tune with the heartbeat of God. Their hearts beat in rhythm with the heart of God. They love what God loves and hate what He hates. This is what makes prophets unique: their heart.

THE HEART OF THE PROPHET

Jesus wept over the city of Jerusalem because they missed their time of visitation. This is the heart of the prophet. The prophet grieves and weeps when people miss what God has for them. This is what breaks the prophet's heart.

When He came near, He beheld the city and wept over it, saying, "If you, even you, had known even today what things would bring you peace! But now they are hidden from your eye.

—LUKE 19:41

WHAT STIRS PROPHETS

Prophets are stirred by other prophets. Prophets benefit from being in a prophetic community. Hearing another prophet's revelation stirs the prophet.

Let two or three prophets speak, and let the others judge. If anything is revealed to another that sits by, let the first keep silent. For you may all prophesy one by one, that all may learn and all may be encouraged.

—1 CORINTHIANS 14:29–31

WHAT MATTERS TO PROPHETS

The things that matter to other people do not matter to prophets. Prophets are concerned about things that others overlook. They are not concerned about carnal things. They are concerned about the things of the Spirit. They are often considered "too deep" by carnal people. They are often considered "troublemakers." Prophets are often considered "crazy" by the disobedient and rebellious.

When Ahab saw Elijah, Ahab said to him, "Are you he that troubles Israel?"

—1 KINGS 18:17

The days of punishment have come; the days of recompense have come. Israel knows! The prophet is a fool; the man of the spirit is insane, because of your great iniquity and great hatred.

—HOSEA 9:7

Judgment (justice), mercy, faith, humility, compassion, love, and truth matter greatly to prophets.

Woe to you, scribes and Pharisees, hypocrites! You tithe mint and dill and cumin, but have neglected the weightier matters of the law: justice and mercy and faith. These you ought to have done without leaving the others undone.

—MATTHEW 23:23

He has told you, O man, what is good—and what does the LORD require of you, but to do justice and to love kindness, and to walk humbly with your God?

—MICAH 6:8

Thus says the LORD of Hosts: Execute true justice, show mercy and compassion, every man to his brother.

—ZECHARIAH 7:9

No one calls for justice, nor does anyone plead for truth. They trust in vanity and speak lies; they conceive mischief and bring forth iniquity.

—ISAIAH 59:4

Character is also important to prophets, not just charisma.

WHAT GIVES PROPHETS JOY

+ Prophets are stirred and joyful when they see revival and glory.
+ They are stirred and joyful when they see God's people moving and advancing.
+ They get excited and joyful when they see the people of God and church breaking through barriers and obstacles.
+ They are stirred and joyful when they see the release of power and miracles.
+ They love to see people saved, delivered, and healed.
+ They love it when backsliders return.
+ They are joyful when they see the things they have been praying for for years manifest.
+ They are joyful when they see the poor and neglected lifted.

+ They are joyful when they see wickedness defeated and righteousness prevailing.

WHAT CAUSES PROPHETS TO GRIEVE

Prophets are grieved and bothered by what others overlook. Prophets
have a sensitivity to the things that grieve God.

+ Prophets are bothered by injustice.
+ Prophets are bothered when things are out of order.
+ Prophets are bothered when the wicked prosper and the
  righteous suffer.
+ Prophets are bothered when the poor and helpless are taken
  advantage of and mistreated.
+ Prophets are bothered when the church is not fulfilling its
  call and purpose.
+ Prophets are bothered when the wrong people are in authority.
+ Prophets are bothered by hypocrisy.
+ Prophets are bothered by false teaching.
+ Prophets are bothered by carnality and apostasy (departure
  from God and the truth).
+ Prophets are grieved by unfairness and abuse.
+ Prophets are grieved by religious tradition and religious
  control.
+ Prophets are grieved by pride, vanity, and arrogance.
+ Prophets are grieved by false worship and wolves (false
  ministries).
+ Prophets are grieved by greed, covetousness, corruption,
  crookedness, and theft.
+ Prophets are grieved by lukewarmness.
+ Prophets are grieved by lying and deception.
+ Prophets are grieved by rebellion, witchcraft, and divination.

These are the things that drive the prophet to prayer. These are the things that drive them to their prayer closets. They pray for change. They cannot stand the way things are. They cry out to God. They weep in their prayer closets. Praying prophets bring change.

> I beheld the transgressors, and was grieved; because they kept not thy word.
>
> —Psalm 119:158, kjv

Be encouraged, prophets. Your prayers make a difference. Joy will come when they are answered.

> But if you will not listen to it, my soul will weep in secret places for your pride; and my eyes will weep sorely and run down with tears, because the flock of the Lord is carried away captive.
>
> —Jeremiah 13:17

Prophets are grieved when there is no love.

Love is important to prophets. You can have activity, but if there is no love, the prophet is grieved. Strife, division, rudeness, and hatred are grievous sins to a prophet. Prophets know that if you don't have love, you don't know God.

> Beloved, let us love one another, for love is of God, and everyone who loves is born of God and knows God. Anyone who does not love does not know God, for God is love.
>
> —1 John 4:7–8

Hardness of heart grieves prophets.

A hard heart is a stony heart. It is a stubborn and unbelieving heart. It is an unyielding heart. Prophets look for soft and tender hearts. Prophets look for broken and contrite hearts.

Jesus became angry at the hardened hearts of the Pharisees.

> When He had looked around at them with anger, being grieved for the hardness of their hearts, He said to the man,

"Stretch your hand forward." He stretched it out, and his hand
was restored as whole as the other.

—MARK 3:5

Being aware of it, Jesus said to them, "Why do you reason
that you have no bread? Do you still not perceive or understand? Are your hearts still hardened?"

—MARK 8:17

Prophets are grieved when there is no prayer.

Prophets know the house of God is a house of prayer. Prophets
call for prayer. Prophets call the church back to prayer.

Even them I will bring to My holy mountain and make them
joyful in My house of prayer. Their burnt offerings and their
sacrifices shall be accepted on My altar; for My house shall be
called a house of prayer for all people.

—ISAIAH 56:7

Prophets are grieved when people miss God.

Jesus wept over Jerusalem because they had missed the time
of their visitation. Prophets know that divine opportunities can be
missed.

They will dash you, and your children within you, to the
ground. They will not leave one stone upon another within
you, because you did not know the time of your visitation.

—LUKE 19:44

WHAT PROPHETS LOVE

Prophets love symbols and symbolic acts.

Symbolism is important to prophets. Sometimes the things of the
Spirit are difficult to articulate with your known language and must
be acted out or relayed through symbols. Symbols can become the
language of the Spirit. The spirit realm is different from the natural
realm, and God gives the prophet ways of relaying a message other
than the limitations of human language.

Then he said, "Open the east window." So he opened it. Then Elisha said, "Shoot." So he shot. Then he said, "The arrow of the deliverance of the LORD, and the arrow of deliverance from Aram; for you must strike Aram in Aphek until you have destroyed them."

—2 KINGS 13:17

Prophets love symbols such as banners, flags, oil, swords, crowns, and so on.

Prophets love the presence of God.

God's presence is the oxygen prophets breathe. They hate it when the presence of God is not in the church. Prophets can't abide programs without presence. They can't stay in places that have become an Ichabod. Prophets don't have a problem being in long services when the presence of God is there.

David, a prophet, loved God's presence. His prophecies came out of being in God's presence.

I have seen You in the sanctuary, to see Your power and Your glory.

—PSALM 63:2

Prophets love and see the bruised and hurting.

Prophets won't disregard them and overlook them. Prophets have an eye to see the broken, bruised, and hurting. They can pick them out of a crowd. They can see those in need of healing and restoration when others overlook them and pass them by.

He won't brush aside the bruised and the hurt and he won't disregard the small and insignificant, but he'll steadily and firmly set things right. He won't tire out and quit. He won't be stopped until he's finished his work—to set things right on earth.

—ISAIAH 42:3–4, THE MESSAGE

Prophets love worship.

Prophets love the glory and presence of God. Prophets are inspirational by nature, and prophets love inspired worship. Prophets love new songs and new sounds. The song of the Lord stirs prophets. Prophets make great worship leaders.

Some of the greatest worshippers in the Bible were prophets. David, Asaph, Heman, are Jeduthun were worshippers that were prophets (1 Chron. 25:1–6). Worship is connected to the spirit of prophecy.

Israel's worship was established by prophets.

> And he set the Levites at the house of the LORD with cymbals, harps, and lyres according to the commandment of David, and Gad the seer of the king, and Nathan the prophet. For the commandment came from the LORD through His prophets.
>
> —2 CHRONICLES 29:25

> I fell at his feet to worship him. But he said to me, "See that you not do that. I am your fellow servant, and of your brothers who hold the testimony of Jesus. Worship God! For the testimony of Jesus is the spirit of prophecy."
>
> —REVELATION 19:10

Worship creates an atmosphere for the spirit of prophecy. Prophets and prophetic people thrive in the atmosphere of worship. Prophets can function as worship leaders, psalmists, and minstrels. They release prophetic sounds and prophetic songs that bring deliverance, healing, restoration, and refreshing.

There are also prophets who operate as seers. Seers have the ability to see into the spirit realm, and then declare what they see. When seers are involved in our worship, they see what is taking place in the spirit realm while we worship and as a result of our worship. Seers have seen angels, smoke, fire, rain, demons, horses, armies, thrones, jewels, judgments, colors, and so on. They can declare what they see to the congregation and encourage the saints to act on what they see. This results in great freedom and breakthroughs.

We need to make room for seers in our worship services. Any believer can see if God permits, but seers are proven prophetic ministries that are recognized by the leadership of the church.

Anointed music and musicians quicken the prophetic word.

> 2 Kings 3:11–16. King Jehoshaphat desired a prophetic word to give him direction. He inquired for a prophet (vs. 11), and Elisha was brought forward. Elisha sought for a minstrel to be played, that the hand of the Lord came upon him" (vs. 15). The anointed music quickened the prophetic word to Elisha, and then he prophesied the Word of the Lord. Even a prophet such as Elisha had to have music to quicken the prophetic word.
>
> 1 Samuel 10:5–6, 10. A company of prophets are seen as coming down a road, preceded by those who played psalterys, tabrets, pipes, and harps. The result was that by the preceding of anointed music, not only did the prophets prophesy, but the spirit of prophecy came upon Saul, and he also prophesied. It was the presence of music that quickened the prophetic word to Saul and the prophets.[1]

Prophets you are not crazy. You are just crazy about praise and worship.

> Praise the LORD! Praise God in His sanctuary; praise Him in the firmament of His power! Praise Him for His mighty acts; praise Him according to His excellent greatness! Praise Him with the sound of the trumpet; praise Him with the lyre and harp! Praise Him with the tambourine and dancing; praise Him with stringed instruments and flute! Praise Him with loud cymbals; praise Him with the clanging cymbals! Let everything that has breath praise the LORD.
>
> —PSALM 150:1–6

Prophets love the dance.

Prophets love the dance because they are people of movement.
God is a God of movement, and anointed movement can release the
blessing of God.

> Miriam the prophetess, the sister of Aaron, took a timbrel in
> her hand, and all the women went out after her with timbrels
> and with dancing.
>
> —EXODUS 15:20

> Then you will go to the Hill of God in Gibeah, where there is
> a Philistine camp. At the entrance to the town you will meet
> a group of prophets coming down from the altar on the hill,
> playing harps, drums, flutes, and lyres. They will be dancing
> and shouting.
>
> —1 SAMUEL 10:5, GNT

> David, wearing only a linen cloth around his waist, danced
> with all his might to honor the LORD.
>
> —2 SAMUEL 6:14

Dancing is a symbol of victory, joy, and celebration. No dancing is
a sign of defeat and mourning.

> Then the virgin shall rejoice in the dance, both young men
> and old together; for I will turn their mourning into joy, and
> will comfort them, and make them rejoice from their sorrow.
>
> —JEREMIAH 31:13

> The joy of our hearts has ceased; our dancing has turned into
> mourning.
>
> —LAMENTATIONS 5:15

Prophets love musical instruments in the praise of God.

Did you know that David made instruments for praise?

> Heman and Jeduthun had with them trumpets and cymbals
> to sound aloud and instruments for sacred song. The sons of
> Jeduthun were appointed to the gate.
>
> —1 CHRONICLES 16:42

Four thousand shall be gatekeepers, and four thousand shall offer praises to the LORD with the instruments that I have made for praise.

—1 CHRONICLES 23:5

Prophets love liberty.

Freedom is the desire of prophets. Prophets hate bondage and control. Prophets hate when the Holy Spirit is quenched. Prophets want God's people to be free and enjoy liberty.

Now the Lord is the Spirit, and where the Spirit of the Lord is, there is liberty (emancipation from bondage, freedom).

—2 CORINTHIANS 3:17, AMP

For freedom Christ freed us. Stand fast therefore and do not be entangled again with the yoke of bondage.

—GALATIANS 5:1

Prophets love rhema.

The Bible is the *logos*. When God quickens a word from the logos, it becomes *rhema*. There are scriptures that are applicable at certain times in your life. Prophets release the rhema. What is God speaking from His Word (logos) today is rhema.

In Greek the word *rhema* means "an utterance." Therefore, the rhema word in biblical terms refers to a portion of Scripture that "speaks" to a believer. Matthew 4:4 is an excellent example of its importance: "Man shall not live by bread alone, but by every word [rhema] that proceeds out of the mouth of God."

To a prophet there is nothing worse than stale preaching and teaching—yesterday's word, yesterday's anointing. Rhema is fresh and applicable in the now season.

We should all love and study the Word (logos). Prophets should study and know the Word (logos), but prophets should release rhema.

Prophets love the deeper things of the Spirit.

Prophets are not shallow. They like depth. They like to understand the deeper things of God. They understand the mysteries of God. They hate shallowness. They are the first to embrace deeper truths. They are called "too deep" by shallow people. Prophets understand that God is greater and deeper than most people understand. Prophets press the church to go deeper, higher, and wider in their understanding of the mysteries of God.

> O LORD, how great are Your works! Your thoughts are very deep.
>
> —PSALM 92:5

> But God has revealed them to us by His Spirit. For the Spirit searches all things, yes, the deep things of God.
>
> —1 CORINTHIANS 2:10

Prophets love the babes.

Although prophets love when the saints mature, they also love the babes. Prophets have a heart for the babes (the childish, unskilled, and untaught). The babes are those with childlike faith. The babes are the humble.

It is much easier to deal with babes than with some people who have been in the church for years. Babes are excited about the new things of the Spirit. Prophets love innocence, purity, and childlike faith.

> At that time Jesus rejoiced in the Holy Spirit and said, "I thank You, O Father, Lord of heaven and earth, because You have hidden these things from the wise and intelligent and revealed them to infants. Yes, Father, for it was Your good pleasure.
>
> —LUKE 10:21

Prophets love the faithful.

Prophets look for the faithful. Prophets love faithfulness. Prophets love the faithful. The faithful are those who are steadfast with God. The faithful are the ones who serve God without compromise. Prophets grieve when there is no faithfulness.

Prophets encourage the faithful. They remind the faithful of God's blessings and faithfulness to them. They encourage the faithful to keep moving ahead in spite of any obstacles and persecutions. Prophets will preach faithfulness.

> Help, LORD, for the godly man comes to an end, for the faithful disappear from sons of men.
>
> —PSALM 12:1

> A faithful man will abound with blessings, but he who makes haste to be rich shall not be innocent.
>
> —PROVERBS 28:20

> Do not fear any of those things which you are about to suffer. Look, the devil is about to throw some of you into prison, that you may be tried, and you will have tribulation for ten days. Be faithful unto death, and I will give you the crown of life.
>
> —REVELATION 2:10

WHAT PROPHETS HATE

Prophets hate injustice and hypocrisy.

> What do you mean that you beat My people to pieces and grind the faces of the poor? says the Lord GOD of Hosts.
>
> —ISAIAH 3:15

> Woe to you, scribes and Pharisees, hypocrites! You devour widows' houses and for pretense make long prayers. Therefore you will receive the greater condemnation.
>
> —MATTHEW 23:14

Prophets hate crookedness.

> They have acted corruptly to Him; they are not His children, but blemished; they are a perverse and crooked generation.
>
> —DEUTERONOMY 32:5

> What is bent cannot be straightened, and what is missing cannot be counted.
>
> —ECCLESIASTES 1:15

> The way of peace they do not know, and there is no justice in their ways; they have made their paths crooked; whoever walks in them does not know peace.
>
> —ISAIAH 59:8

Prophets hate compromise.

Prophets see things black and white. There are no gray areas for prophets. They hate mixture. They often get in trouble for their stand.

> Ephraim mixes himself with the people, Ephraim is a cake not turned.
>
> —HOSEA 7:8

Prophets would rather walk alone than compromise. But they are never really alone, because they are the friends of God.

> Look to Abraham your father and to Sarah who bore you; for I called him alone, and blessed him, and multiplied him.
>
> —ISAIAH 51:2

Prophets hate mixture.

Mixtures such as…

- Law and grace
- Righteousness and unrighteousness
- Flesh and the Spirit
- Truth and tradition
- Church and the world

+ Light and darkness
+ Clean and unclean

…are revolting to prophets.

> Your silver has become dross, your wine mixed with water.
> —Isaiah 1:22

> They serve in a sanctuary that is an example and shadow of the heavenly one, as Moses was instructed by God when he was about to make the tabernacle, "See that you make all things according to the pattern shown you on the mountain."
> —Hebrews 8:5

> For the law is a shadow of the good things to come, and not the very image of those things. It could never by the same sacrifices, which they offer continually year after year, perfect those who draw near.
> —Hebrews 10:1

> Does a spring yield at the same opening sweet and bitter water?
> —James 3:11

Prophets hate a form of godliness with no power.

> Having a form of godliness, but denying its power. Turn away from such people.
> —2 Timothy 3:5

> For [although] they hold a form of piety (true religion), they deny and reject and are strangers to the power of it [their conduct belies the genuineness of their profession]. Avoid [all] such people [turn away from them].
> —2 Timothy 3:5, AMP

> They will go on pretending to be devoted to God, but they will refuse to let that "devotion" change the way they live. Stay away from these people!
> —2 Timothy 3:5, ERV

Prophets hate the traditions of men.

Prophets hate the traditions of men that make void the Word of God. Prophets will oppose anything that prevents God's people from obeying Him, including tradition. Prophets will oppose these traditions and warn people of the dangers of religious tradition.

> But He answered them, "Why do you also violate the commandment of God by your tradition?"
>
> —MATTHEW 15:3

> Making the word of God of no effect through your tradition, which you have delivered. And you do many similar things.
>
> —MARK 7:13

> Beware lest anyone captivate you through philosophy and vain deceit, in the tradition of men and the elementary principles of the world, and not after Christ.
>
> —COLOSSIANS 2:8

Prophets hate religious control.

It is wrong for leaders to use prophecy to pronounce judgments (doom and gloom) on people because they do not agree with them. This is a manifestation of control, and true prophets will cry against it. Prophets do not manipulate and control people through a word. This is unjust and will grieve and anger a true prophet.

There is no place for rudeness and arrogance in the prophetic ministry. Prophets can be firm, but all things must be done in love. There is no place for control, manipulation, and domination in the prophetic ministry.

> If I speak with the tongues of men and of angels, and have not love, I have become as sounding brass or a clanging cymbal. If I have the gift of prophecy, and understand all mysteries and all knowledge, and if I have all faith, so that I could remove mountains, and have not love, I am nothing.
>
> —1 CORINTHIANS 13:1–2

It is not conceited (arrogant and inflated with pride); it is not rude (unmannerly) and does not act unbecomingly. Love (God's love in us) does not insist on its own rights or its own way, for it is not self-seeking; it is not touchy or fretful or resentful; it takes no account of the evil done to it [it pays no attention to a suffered wrong].

—1 CORINTHIANS 13:5, AMP

Prophets hate witchcraft.

Witchcraft is a work of the flesh, and it is also a demon. Witchcraft is domination, intimidation, manipulation, sorcery, divination, enchantment, spells, hexes, vexes, and legalism. Prophets will discern it and challenge it.

Then I will cut off sorceries from your hand, and you will no longer have fortune-tellers.

—MICAH 5:12

Prophets develop a perfect hatred for evil and wickedness.

Do I not hate those, O LORD, who hate You? And do I not abhor those who rise up against You? I hate them with perfect hatred; I count them my enemies. Search me, O God, and know my heart; try me, and know my concerns.

—PSALM 139:21–23

You have loved righteousness and hated wickedness; therefore God, Your God, has anointed You with the oil of gladness more than Your companions.

—HEBREWS 1:9

Prophets hate maintaining things.

If you give them something to maintain, they will want to improve it, change it, renew it, enlarge it, or simply quit. Prophets don't do well in churches that are only maintaining and not changing, improving, and growing.

Prophets hate "slight healing."

Prophets don't believe in putting a Band-Aid on a deep wound. Don't say, "All is well," when all is not well.

> They have healed also the brokenness of the daughter of My people superficially, saying, "Peace, peace," when there is no peace.
>
> —JEREMIAH 6:14

> They treat the wound of my people as if it were nothing: "All is well, all is well," they insist, when in fact nothing is well.
>
> —JEREMIAH 6:14, CEB

Prophets hate ignorance.

What really bugs a prophet is when people reject knowledge. This includes leadership, churches, and ministries that refuse truth and refuse to grow in knowledge. The knowledge of God is important to prophets.

> Therefore my people are gone into captivity, because they have no knowledge: and their honourable men are famished, and their multitude dried up with thirst.
>
> —ISAIAH 5:13

> My people are destroyed for lack of knowledge. Because you have rejected knowledge, I will reject you from being My priest. And because you have forgotten the law of your God, I will also forget your children.
>
> —HOSEA 4:6

Prophets hate lip service.

Lip service is verbal expression of agreement or allegiance, unsupported by real conviction or action; it is hypocritical respect. Prophets hate when people say but do not do.

> Why do you call Me, "Lord, Lord," and not do what I say?
>
> —LUKE 6:46

Therefore, whatever they tell you to observe, that observe and do, but do not do their works. For they speak, but do nothing.

—MATTHEW 23:3

These people draw near to Me with their mouth, and honor Me with their lips, but their heart is far from Me.

—MATTHEW 15:8

Prophets hate flattery.

Flattery is excessive and insincere praise, especially that given to further one's own interests. Prophets don't flatter. Prophets speak truth. Prophets don't come to "butter you up."

They speak empty words, each with his own neighbor; they speak with flattering lips and a double heart.

—PSALM 12:2

For there shall be no more any vain vision or flattering divination within the house of Israel.

—EZEKIEL 12:24

Prophets hate respect of persons.

This one really bugs prophets.

You shall not show partiality in judgment, but you shall hear the small as well as the great. You shall not be afraid in any man's presence, for the judgment is God's. The case that is too hard for you, you shall bring it to me, and I will hear it.

—DEUTERONOMY 1:17

My brothers, have faith in our Lord Jesus Christ, the Lord of glory, without partiality.

—JAMES 2:1

But if you show partiality, you are committing sin and are convicted by the law as sinners.

—JAMES 2:9

Prophets hate thievery.

Jesus drove the thieves out of the temple. This is the anger of the prophet. Prophets hate when the temple becomes a house of merchandise. This really bugs prophets. Prophets want the thieves out of the temple. They hate thievery and robbery.

> Woe to the bloody city! it is all full of lies and robbery; the prey departeth not.
> —NAHUM 3:1, KJV

> He said to them, "It is written, 'My house shall be called a house of prayer,' but you have made it 'a den of thieves.'"
> —MATTHEW 21:13

Prophets hate slander.

Slander is another thing that bugs prophets. Gossip, backbiting, rumors, and talebearing are sins that need to be exposed and stopped. Prophets can hear slander. They can hear the secret counsel of the wicked. They hate slander against God's leaders, His appointed. Prophets will expose slander. Slander has destroyed ministries, churches, leaders, and so many more.

> For I have heard the slander of many; fear was on every side; while they took counsel together against me, they planned to take away my life.
> —PSALM 31:13

> They all are stubborn rebels walking about practicing slander. They are bronze and iron; they all are corrupters.
> —JEREMIAH 6:28

> Let everyone be on guard against his neighbor, and do not trust in any brother; for every brother supplants, and every neighbor walks about with slanders.
> —JEREMIAH 9:4

Slander and evil speaking have brought much damage to leaders, churches, people, and relationships. It is an evil that must be rooted out. Prophets can detect slander, will pray against it, and help root it out. Slander and evil speaking reflect the condition of the heart. From the abundance of the heart the mouth speaks. Evil people cannot speak good things. Prophets wonder why this bothers them so much. The answer is, "Because it is evil."

> You let loose your mouth to evil, and your tongue is bound to deceit. You sit and speak against your brother; you accuse your own mother's son.
>
> —PSALM 50:19–20

> The tongue is a fire, a world of evil. The tongue is among the parts of the body, defiling the whole body, and setting the course of nature on fire, and it is set on fire by hell.
>
> —JAMES 3:6

> A perverse man sows strife, and a whisperer separates the best of friends.
>
> —PROVERBS 16:28

Prophets hate empty religion.

They challenge the church when it moves away from God's power and replaces it with man's agenda, human strength, and earthly wisdom.

Prophets hate when the name of the Lord is blasphemed.

To blaspheme means to dishonor and insult. Prophets have a passion for the name of the Lord to be honored and exalted.

> O God, how long will the adversary scorn? Will the enemy blaspheme Your name forever?
>
> —PSALM 74:10

> Remember this, that the enemy has scorned, O LORD, and that the foolish people have blasphemed Your name.
>
> —PSALM 74:18

> Now therefore, what do I have here, says the LORD, seeing that My people have been taken away for nothing? Those who

rule over them make them wail, says the LORD, and My name is continually blasphemed all day long.

—ISAIAH 52:5

The name of God is blasphemed among the Gentiles because of you.

—ROMANS 2:24

Do they not blaspheme that worthy name by which you are called?

—JAMES 2:7

Prophets hate false discipleship.

In other words, prophets hate when leaders make people their disciples instead of making them disciples of Christ.

Woe to you, scribes and Pharisees, hypocrites! You travel sea and land to make one proselyte, and when he becomes one, you make him twice as much a son of hell as yourselves.

—MATTHEW 23:15

Prophets hate the false.

A part of the prophet's ministry is to discern the true from the false. Prophets hate lies and deception.

False prophets are greedy. True prophets hate greed.

False prophets are covetous. True prophets hate covetousness.

False prophets are abusive. True prophets hate abuse.

False prophets are controlling. True prophets hate control.

False prophets are arrogant. True prophets are humble.

False prophets cannot produce good fruit. True prophets look for fruit.

False prophets are deceptive. True prophets discern deception.

Beware of false prophets who come to you in sheep's clothing, but inwardly they are ravenous wolves. 16 You will know them by their fruit. Do men gather grapes from thorns, or figs from thistles?

—MATTHEW 7:15–16

For you permit it if a man brings you into bondage, if a man devours you, if a man takes from you, if a man exalts himself, or if a man strikes you on the face.

—2 Corinthians 11:20

Prophets cannot abide false shepherds, false apostles, false prophets, false teachers, false bishops, false brethren, false accusers, and false witnesses. False doctrine will really bug prophets.

Prophets cannot abide false ministries. They will vex and upset prophets. Prophets want to rescue people from false ministries. A prophet will tell you to "leave." A prophet will help you get out.

Transgressing, and lying against the LORD, and departing away from our God, speaking oppression and revolt, conceiving and uttering from the heart words of falsehood.

—Isaiah 59:13

My people have been lost sheep. Their shepherds have caused them to go astray; they have turned them away on the mountains. They have gone from mountain to hill and have forgotten their resting place.

—Jeremiah 50:6

Son of man, prophesy against the shepherds of Israel. Prophesy and say to those shepherds, Thus says the Lord God: Woe to the shepherds of Israel who feed themselves! Should not the shepherds feed the flock?

—Ezekiel 34:2

WHAT PROPHETS DESIRE

Prophets desire demonstration of the Spirit and power.

Prophets are not impressed with enticing words of man's wisdom. Prophets want a move of the Spirit in demonstration and power. Man's doctrines and philosophies don't impress prophets. Prophets desire words that release power, healing, deliverance, and miracles.

My speech and my preaching was not with enticing words
of man's wisdom, but in demonstration of the Spirit and of
power.

—1 CORINTHIANS 2:4

I didn't speak my message with persuasive intellectual argu-
ments. I spoke my message with a show of spiritual power.

—1 CORINTHIANS 2:4, GW

Prophets desire to see God's power and glory.

I have seen You in the sanctuary, to see Your power and Your
glory.

—PSALM 63:2

David was a prophet. You can learn a lot about the heart of a
prophet by studying David. David's desire was to see God's power and
glory. David yearned for the presence of God.

Prophets enjoy a lifestyle of power and glory. Prophets want
everyone to experience God's power and glory. They cry out, "Lord,
show me Your glory!"

Then Moses said, "I pray, show me Your glory."

—EXODUS 33:18

In the year that king Uzziah died I saw the LORD sitting on
a throne, high and lifted up, and His train filled the temple.

—ISAIAH 6:1

Prophets desire to behold the beauty of the Lord.

One thing I have asked from the LORD, that will I seek after—
for me to dwell in the house of the LORD all the days of my life,
to see the beauty of the LORD, and to inquire in His temple.

—PSALM 27:4

Prophets love the beauty of God. They want everyone to experience His beauty. God's beauty is His perfection and glory. This was
the desire of David, who was a prophet.

Prophets desire the judgments of the Lord.

> The fear of the LORD is clean, enduring forever; the judgments of the LORD are true and righteous altogether. More to be desired are they than gold, yes, than much fine gold; sweeter also than honey and the honeycomb.
>
> —PSALM 19:9–10

Prophets love the fear of the Lord and the judgments (ordinances) of the Lord. They desire them more than gold. They are sweeter than honey. Prophets seek and dig into the judgments (ordinances) of God. God's judgments are "a great deep."

> Your righteousness is like the great mountains, Your judgments like the great deep.
>
> —PSALM 36:6

Prophets desire truth in the inward parts.

> You desire truth in the inward parts, and in the hidden part You make me to know wisdom.
>
> —PSALM 51:6

Prophets want truth in the inward parts. The hidden part of man is the prophet's focus. Prophets desire what God desires.

Prophets desire to know the will of God.

> For this reason we also, since the day we heard it, do not cease to pray for you and to ask that you may be filled with the knowledge of His will in all wisdom and spiritual understanding.
>
> —COLOSSIANS 1:9

Prophets want to know God's will. They want to be filled with wisdom and understanding of His will. They desire for God's people to know His will and be filled with wisdom and spiritual understanding.

Prophets desire sincere and pure devotion to Christ.

Prophets desire a sincere and pure devotion to Christ. They do not want to see the people of God corrupted from the simplicity of Christ. Simplicity is sincerity. Prophets want to see an uncorrupted devotion to Christ.

> But [now] I am fearful, lest that even as the serpent beguiled Eve by his cunning, so your minds may be corrupted and seduced from wholehearted and sincere and pure devotion to Christ.
>
> —2 CORINTHIANS 11:3, AMP

Prophets desire to see God pleased.

Prophets are grieved when God is not pleased. Prophets rejoice when God is pleased. Prophets will reveal what pleases God and what displeases Him.

> But with many of them God was not well pleased, and they were overthrown in the wilderness.
>
> —1 CORINTHIANS 10:5

> Finally, brothers, we urge and exhort you by the Lord Jesus, that as you have learned from us how you ought to walk and to please God, you should excel more and more.
>
> —1 THESSALONIANS 4:1

4

THE REWARDS OF A PROPHET

He who receives a prophet in the name of a
prophet shall receive a prophet's reward.

—MATTHEW 10:41

LOVE PROPHETS. PROPHETS are special. God told me years ago to be a friend to prophets. This is why I love them, encourage them, and bless them.

God rewards those who receive and bless prophets. Those who are hospitable to prophets get God's attention. The treatment of prophets is a sign of a person's heart toward God. Prophets are sent representatives. Rejecting prophets is tantamount to rejecting God. Favor, blessing, promotion, and financial breakthrough are some of the blessings that come into your life when you receive a prophet of God.

In this chapter I am going to expand on the prophet's reward that you can receive as you welcome the ministry of prophets.

ENCOURAGEMENT

Prophets are great encouragers. Prophets love to encourage others. This is one of the assignments of prophets. They will encourage people others have forgotten. If you need encouragement, get around prophets.

In Acts 4:36 Barnabas is called "the son of prophecy." Some translations will call him "the son of encouragement." The words in these verses for "prophecy," "encouragement," and "exhort" are so closely related that they actually can be translated either way.

> Judas and Silas, being prophets themselves, exhorted the brothers with many words and strengthened them.
>
> —ACTS 15:32

But Joshua the son of Nun, who stands before you, he shall go in. Encourage him, for he will cause Israel to inherit it.

—DEUTERONOMY 1:38

Prophets bring encouragement through prophecy, singing, preaching, teaching, and counseling.

Prophets encourage you to seek God, not wizards.

Seek God. Don't seek after wizards that peep and mutter. Don't seek after those with familiar spirits. This is the cry of the prophet.

And when they shall say unto you, Seek unto them that have familiar spirits, and unto wizards that peep, and that mutter: should not a people seek unto their God? for the living to the dead?

—ISAIAH 8:19, KJV

Or a charmer, or a consulter with familiar spirits, or a wizard, or a necromancer. For all that do these things are an abomination unto the LORD: and because of these abominations the LORD thy God doth drive them out from before thee.

—DEUTERONOMY 18:11–12, KJV

Prophets speak to and encourage the weary.

Prophets love ministering to the weary. Prophets are called and sent to the weary. Prophets have compassion and love for the weary. Prophets bring encouragement to the weary. They bring refreshing to the tired. If you are tired and weary, you need to get around the prophets.

Prophets can identify weariness and discouragement quickly. They are sensitive to it. The weary are the sad, the tired, the faint, and the discouraged.

The Lord GOD has given me the tongue of the learned, that I may know how to sustain him who is weary with a word;

He awakens me morning by morning; He awakens my ear to
listen as the learned.

—Isaiah 50:4

**Prophets are needed when there is weakness and
discouragement.**

The Jews were weak and discouraged when they were rebuilding
the temple. God raised up Haggai and Zechariah to encourage them
and strengthen them. They were able to finish the work with the help
of the prophets.

> Now the prophets, Haggai and Zechariah the son of Iddo,
> prophesied to the Jews that were in Judah and Jerusalem
> in the name of the God of Israel who was over them. Then
> Zerubbabel the son of Shealtiel and Joshua the son of
> Jozadak rose up and began to build the house of God which
> is at Jerusalem, and the prophets of God were with them,
> helping them.... The rebuilding by the elders of the Jews pros-
> pered through the prophesying of Haggai the prophet and
> Zechariah the son of Iddo. And they built, and finished it,
> according to the decree of the God of Israel and according to
> the decrees of Cyrus, Darius, and Artaxerxes king of Persia.
> This temple was finished on the third day of the month Adar
> during the sixth year of the reign of Darius the king.
>
> —Ezra 5:1–2; 6:14–15

CONVICTION

Prophets know the power of conviction. Isaiah was convicted when he
saw the glory of the Lord (Isa. 6:5–7). David was convicted when he
was challenged by the prophet Nathan. Without conviction there is
no change. Conviction is the grace of the prophet. Their words bring
conviction. They operate in the power of conviction.

When they heard this, they were stung in the heart and said to Peter and to the rest of the apostles, "Brothers, what shall we do?"

—ACTS 2:37

But if all prophesy [giving inspired testimony and interpreting the divine will and purpose] and an unbeliever or untaught outsider comes in, he is told of his sin and reproved and convicted and convinced by all, and his defects and needs are examined (estimated, determined) and he is called to account by all.

—1 CORINTHIANS 14:24, AMP

HOPE

Prophets bring hope. Prophets can step into hopeless situations and prophesy a turnaround. Prophets can see beyond hopeless situations. They can see restoration. They can see change. Elijah was sent into a hopeless situation when he went to the widow of Zarephath and caused her to receive a miracle and a turnaround. If you are feeling hopeless and discouraged, get around prophets.

Then He said to me, "Son of man, these bones are the whole house of Israel. They say, 'Our bones are dried up, and our hope is lost. We are cut off completely.' Therefore prophesy and say to them, Thus says the Lord God: Pay attention, O My people, I will open your graves and cause you to come up out of your graves and bring you into the land of Israel."

—EZEKIEL 37:11–12

Prophets prophesy divine intervention.

God intervenes in the affairs of men. Prayer brings His intervention. He intervenes with judgment, salvation, and deliverance. Prophets prophesy His intervention.

Oh, that You would rend the heavens and come down, that the mountains might shake at Your presence.

—ISAIAH 64:1

CONFIRMATION

Prophets bring confirmation. Prophets love to confirm. They love to say, "This is of God." Whatever God does can be confirmed. *To confirm* means to establish the truth or correctness of something. Prophets validate. Churches need validation. People need validation. It is not the validation of men but the validation of God.

> Judas and Silas, being prophets themselves, exhorted the brothers with many words and strengthened them.
>
> —ACTS 15:32

Prophets know when "it's not of God"!

IMPARTATION

Prophets impart. Presbyteries are elders who prophesy. The leadership of the church should be prophetic. Timothy received a gift through the laying on of hands of the elders with prophecy. When prophets are a part of ordinations, there is a powerful release of grace and gifting. Prophets don't just have ceremony; they have life-changing services. If you want powerful ordinations, include the prophets.

> Do not neglect the gift which is in you, [that special inward endowment] which was directly imparted to you [by the Holy Spirit] by prophetic utterance when the elders laid their hands upon you [at your ordination].
>
> —1 TIMOTHY 4:14, AMP

EARLY WARNING

An early warning system is a condition, system, or series of procedures indicating a potential development or impending problem; a network of sensing devices, such as satellites or radar, for detecting an enemy attack in time to take defensive or counteroffensive measures. Prophets can see trouble coming before it arrives and can warn us of impending danger or judgment. They are the early warning system of the church.

> The king of Israel sent word to the place of which the man of God spoke. He warned him and was on his guard there more than once.
>
> —2 KINGS 6:10

> Son of man, I have made you a watchman to the house of Israel. Whenever you hear the word from My mouth, then warn them from Me.
>
> —EZEKIEL 3:17

Prophets are the trumpets of God.

The prophet's voice is a trumpet. God has called His prophets to be trumpets. Prophets are the trumpet of God. Trumpets cannot make any sound without breath blowing through them, and the Greek word translated as both "spirit" and "wind" in the Bible is *pneuma*, meaning wind, air, and breath. The holy breath of God, the Spirit of God, moves through prophets when they speak.

Trumpets were used to gather and to warn. Trumpets announce new seasons. They must give a clear sound so people know what is being sounded. When people hear the trumpet they will respond. The voice of God is like a trumpet. A trumpet is known by its clarity of sound.

> God went up with a shout, the LORD with the sound of a trumpet.
>
> —PSALM 47:5

> Blow the trumpet at the New Moon, at the full moon on our feast day.
>
> —PSALM 81:3

> Blow the trumpet in Zion, sanctify a fast, call a solemn assembly.
>
> —JOEL 2:15, KJV

Prophets hear and sound the alarm.

Alarms are sounded when there is imminent danger. Prophets are alarms. They are the alarm clocks of the church. Alarm clocks are needed to wake up the sleeping.

> Blow the ram's horn in Zion, sound the alarm on My holy mountain! All the inhabitants of the earth will tremble, because the day of the Lord has come, because it is near.
>
> —JOEL 2:1

There is no remedy if you reject the warnings of prophets.

A remedy is something that corrects an evil, fault, or error.

> But they continued to jest regarding the messengers of God, despising His word and making fun of His prophets until the wrath of the LORD came up against His people, until there was no remedy.
>
> —2 CHRONICLES 36:16

> He who is often reproved, yet hardens his neck, will suddenly be destroyed, and that without remedy.
>
> —PROVERBS 29:1

Pilate's wife

Pontius Pilate's wife had a dream about Christ, and she warned Pilate to have nothing to do with Jesus, a just man. God can use dreams to warn us. Pilate did not heed the dream of his wife, but instead he turned Jesus over to the Jews to be crucified.

> When he was sitting on the judgment seat, his wife sent word to him, "Have nothing to do with that righteous Man, for I have suffered much today in a dream on account of Him."
>
> —MATTHEW 27:19

Pilate was guilty because he was warned. He knew that Christ was innocent. He knew Christ was delivered to him because of envy. He was more intent on pleasing the mob than doing what was right.

Pilate is an example of someone who was warned but does the opposite. Pilate is listed with Herod, the Gentiles, and the people of Israel in gathering together against Christ. He is classified as an enemy of Christ.

> Indeed, both Herod and Pontius Pilate, with the Gentiles and the people of Israel, were assembled together against Your holy Son Jesus whom You have anointed.
> —ACTS 4:27

The story of Pilate is tragic. It shows the tragedy of not having the courage to heed a warning. Don't ignore warnings. A warning can save your life and prevent you from doing something tragic.

PRESERVATION AND PROTECTION

> By a prophet the LORD brought Israel up from Egypt, and by a prophet was he preserved.
> —HOSEA 12:13

Prophets preserve and protect. God uses prophets to lead His people and to protect them. Prophets are very protective of the ones they have been assigned to.

Hosea 12:13 reveals to us that one of the major functions of the prophet's ministry is preservation. Israel was delivered from Egypt through the ministry of Moses. Israel was preserved through the intercession of Moses (Num. 14:11–20).

Preserve means to keep from harm, damage, danger, or evil. It also means to protect or to save. In Hebrew the root word is *shamar*. *Shamar* means to hedge about (as with thorns), to guard, to protect, to watch, and to keep. The word *shamar* is first used in Scripture in Genesis 2:15, where Adam is told to keep (*shamar*) the garden. It is also mentioned in Genesis 4:9, where Cain asks God if he is his brother's keeper (*shamar*).

This word *shamar* emphasizes the protective element of the prophet's mantle. The preserving and guarding aspect of the prophet's ministry is needed in every local church. Many well-meaning pastors have suffered unnecessarily due to the lack of understanding this aspect of the ministry of the prophet. The *shamar* aspect of the prophet's ministry is one of the most important ones, and it will benefit the church greatly.

The local church is kept safe through prophetic intercession, prophetic discernment, prophetic praise, prophetic preaching, prophetic teaching, and prophetic worship. This is how the church is best defended. Without a revelation of the *shamar* aspect of the prophetic ministry, a local church will suffer from many attacks that could be averted.

A CALL TO A HIGHER PLACE

Prophets call us to the mountain. They call us higher. They call us to ascend. The mountain is Zion, the mountain of God. It is the place of God's presence and dominion. It is the place of glory. It is the place of holiness. It is a place of teaching and revelation. Prophets challenge us to leave the low places of the flesh and come to the high place of the Spirit.

> They will call the peoples to the mountain; there they will offer sacrifices of righteousness, for they will draw out the abundance of the seas and the treasures hid in the sand.
>
> —DEUTERONOMY 33:19

> Many people shall go and say, "Come, and let us go up to the mountain of the LORD, to the house of the God of Jacob, and He will teach us of His ways, and we will walk in His paths." For out of Zion shall go forth the law, and the word of the LORD from Jerusalem.
>
> —ISAIAH 2:3

GROWTH

Prophets stretch us. Prophets will challenge the church in the area of faith. Prophets will encourage the saints to "believe God for greater things." Prophets hate doubt and unbelief. They speak things that require you to believe. They stretch your faith with the word of the Lord.

Prophets can speak things that are sometimes hard to believe. The prophet moves us into areas that are impossible with man but possible with God. God uses prophets to push us past our comfort levels.

Prophets will sometimes speak words that seem so impossible that they will say, "Did I just say that?"

Prophets help us go through God's chastening (correction).

God's discipline is important to prophets. Prophets lift up the hands that hang down and strengthen the feeble knees. We all need encouragement when we are going through correction. Prophets are good at helping us endure God's correction in our lives.

> Now no chastening for the present seemeth to be joyous, but grievous: nevertheless afterward it yieldeth the peaceable fruit of righteousness unto them which are exercised thereby. Wherefore lift up the hands which hang down, and the feeble knees; and make straight paths for your feet, lest that which is lame be turned out of the way; but let it rather be healed.
>
> —HEBREWS 12:11–13, KJV

> Those whom I love, I rebuke and discipline. Therefore be zealous and repent.
>
> —REVELATION 3:19

Prophets challenge us to make a decision.

Elijah, asked Israel, "How long will you stay between two opinions?" Elijah challenged them to make a decision. A double-minded man is unstable in all his ways (James 1:8).

Eliyahu stepped forward before all the people and said, "How long are you going to jump back and forth between two positions? If ADONAI is God, follow him; but if it's Ba'al, follow him!" The people answered him not a word.

—1 KINGS 18:21, CJB

Come close to God, and he will come close to you. Clean your hands, sinners; and purify your hearts, you double-minded people!

—JAMES 4:8

I call heaven and earth to witnesses against you this day, that I have set before you life and death, blessing and curse. Therefore choose life, that both you and your descendants may live.

—DEUTERONOMY 30:19

Prophets challenge our comfort zone.

Amos gave a word to those who were at ease in Zion. They were comfortable in their sin and rebellion. They felt safe and secure in their disobedience. They were living an easy life without any concern for others who were downtrodden and oppressed.

Woe to those who are at ease in Zion and to those on the mountain of Samaria who are careless and feel secure, the notable men of the chief [because chosen by God] of the nations, to whom the house of Israel comes!

—AMOS 6:1, AMP

Who lie upon beds of ivory, and lounge on their couches, eating lambs from the flock and calves from the stall.

—AMOS 6:4

FORESIGHT

Prophets can see the end from the beginning. Prophets know where people, churches, cities, and nations are headed based on their decisions. They will know the end. They will know where you are heading.

They will know where you are going. Prophets encourage and warn people to make the right decisions so their end can be blessed. They try to turn you around if you are heading to a bad ending.

> Declaring the end from the beginning, and from ancient times the things that are not yet done, saying, "My counsel shall stand, and I will do all My good pleasure."
>
> —Isaiah 46:10

Before God acts, He shows His prophets. Prophets will see it and pray it before it happens. This is heaven working with earth.

> Surely the Lord God does nothing without revealing His purpose to His servants the prophets.
>
> —Amos 3:7

Prophets help keep us poised for the future.

The future is not our enemy. Prophets help keep us poised for the future. Prophets will not let you get stuck in the past. Prophets bring hope for the future. Prophets understand destiny and purpose. They will help us not to fear the future or to remain stuck in the past.

> "For I know the plans I have for you," declares the Lord, "plans to prosper you and not to harm you, plans to give you hope and a future."
>
> —Jeremiah 29:11, niv

> For the Lord God is a Sun and Shield; the Lord bestows [present] grace and favor and [future] glory (honor, splendor, and heavenly bliss)! No good thing will He withhold from those who walk uprightly.
>
> —Psalm 84:11, amp

> For surely there is a latter end [a future and a reward], and your hope and expectation shall not be cut off.
>
> —Proverbs 23:18, amp

Prophets are concerned about your future.

Prophets want to know where you are heading. They want to know what decisions you are making now that affect your future. They want to know if you are fulfilling destiny. (See Jeremiah 29:11.)

DISCERNING OF TIMES AND SEASONS

Prophets know the seasons. It is important to know the seasons. Seasons change, and there is a time and season for every purpose under heaven. Prophets are sensitive to changing seasons. They can minister to you when your season is changing.

> Winter, spring, summer, and fall,
> The prophet will sense and know them all.

> To every thing there is a season, and a time to every purpose under the heaven.
> —ECCLESIASTES 3:1

Prophets understand times and seasons.

Prophets are concerned about God's purposes and the timing to fulfill them.

> He changes times and seasons; he deposes kings and raises up others. He gives wisdom to the wise and knowledge to the discerning.
> —DANIEL 2:21, NIV

PURIFICATION

Prophets deal with the inward parts (the kidneys). The reins (inward parts) are symbolized in Scripture by the kidneys. Kidneys help remove waste from your system. They are a symbol of purification and purity.

What is in your kidneys (heart, reins, mind, inward parts)? I am not talking about the physical kidneys, but the reins, the heart, that which the kidneys represent. Prophets are concerned about your inward parts, your kidneys. Let all uncleanness be removed from your kidneys, and let your inward parts be pure.

Prophets know the outward is only a manifestation of the inward.

> And I will kill her children with death, and all the congregations shall know that I AM he that searches the kidneys and hearts, and I will give unto each one of you according to your works.
>
> —REVELATION 2:23, JUB

> I will bless the LORD, who gives me counsel: my kidneys also instruct me in the night seasons.
>
> —PSALM 16:7, JUB

> Praise [bless] the LORD because he advises me. Even at night, I feel his leading [my innards instruct me].
>
> —PSALM 16:7, EXB

> For there is no faithfulness in their mouth; their inward part is very wickedness; their throat is an open sepulchre; they flatter with their tongue.
>
> —PSALM 5:9, KJV

SUCCESSFUL NEGOTIATION WITH GOD

Prophets negotiate with God. In Exodus 32 at the end of the "golden calf" incident, Moses really persuaded God to change His mind. The prophet can ask the Lord to change His mind when it comes to judgment. Moses did it, and God spared Israel.

Abraham also negotiated with God for Lot and his family before God destroyed Sodom.

> "Suppose there were five less than the fifty righteous. Will You destroy all the city for lack of five?" And He said, "If I find forty-five there, I will not destroy it."
>
> —GENESIS 18:28

This is the power of the prophet. This is the kind of relationship prophets have with God. The prophet is the friend of God.

MINISTRY OF THE WORD AND PRAYER

Prophets speak and pray. Jesus gave the disciples the word and prayed for them. Prophets don't just drop words. They also pray for those who receive the word. This does not mean prophets will pray for everyone they give a word to, but there are people they are assigned to minister to and pray for. Demons will fight the prophetic word, and the prayers of the prophet will help overcome the opposition of the enemy, who comes to hinder and delay the prophetic word.

> For I have given them the words which You gave Me. They have received them and certainly know that I came from You, and they have believed that You sent Me. I pray for them. I do not pray for the world, but for those whom You have given Me. For they are Yours.
>
> —JOHN 17:8–9

INSTRUCTION

Prophets can give you instructions that will cause breakthrough. Prophets hear from God and release unusual instructions.

Prophet, don't be surprised when God gives you His wisdom when you are confronted with impossible situations. Desperate people will pull on your gift.

> Elisha said to her, "What shall I do for you? Tell me, what do you have in the house?" She said, "Your servant has nothing in the house except a jar of oil." Then he said, "Go, ask for vessels from all your neighbors, empty vessels and not just a few. Then go in, shut the door behind you and your sons, and pour the oil into all these vessels. When each is full, set it aside." So she left him and shut the door behind her and her sons, and they kept bringing vessels to her, and she kept pouring. When the vessels were full, she said to her son, "Bring me another vessel." But he said to her, "There is not another vessel." And the oil ceased. Then she went and told the man

of God. And he said, "Go, sell the oil, and pay your debt, and you and your children can live on the rest."

—2 KINGS 4:2–7

UNCOVERING OF ROOT PROBLEMS

Prophets get to the root of the problem. What is the root of the problem? What is hidden beneath the surface? Roots are hidden, but they are the source of what is growing. John came to lay the ax to the root.

Is the root rebellion? Is the root fear? Is the root unforgiveness? Is the root bitterness? Is the root pride? Is the root rejection? Is the plant planted by God?

Prophets don't deal with surface issues. Prophets deal with root issues.

> See, I have this day set you over the nations and over the king-
> doms, to root out and to pull down, to destroy and to throw
> down, to build and to plant.
>
> —JEREMIAH 1:10

> Even now the axe is put to the tree roots. Therefore, every
> tree which does not bear good fruit is cut down and thrown
> into the fire.
>
> —MATTHEW 3:10

> But He answered, "Every plant which My heavenly Father
> has not planted will be uprooted."
>
> —MATTHEW 15:13

SENSITIVITY TO THE SPIRIT OF GOD

Prophets know when the Holy Spirit is grieved. The Holy Spirit can be grieved and vexed. Ephesians 4:30 in the Message Bible says, "Don't grieve God. Don't break his heart. His Holy Spirit, moving and breathing in you, is the most intimate part of your life, making you fit for himself. Don't take such a gift for granted."

Prophets are grieved when the Holy Spirit is grieved.

> And do not grieve the Holy Spirit of God, in whom you are
> sealed for the day of redemption.
>
> —EPHESIANS 4:30

> But they rebelled and grieved His Holy Spirit; therefore, He
> turned Himself to be their enemy, and He fought against
> them.
>
> —ISAIAH 63:10

Prophets also know when the glory is departed (Ichabod). It is
amazing how some people can carry on after the glory has departed.
The prophet cannot act as if the glory is still there when it has
departed. Ezekiel saw the glory lift and depart. It is a sad day when
the glory has departed.

> Then the glory of the LORD departed from off the threshold of
> the temple and stood over the cherubim.
>
> —EZEKIEL 10:18

> And she named the child Ichabod, saying, "The glory is
> departed from Israel," because the ark of God was taken, and
> because of her father-in-law and her husband.
>
> —1 SAMUEL 4:21

EXPOSING OF THE PLANS OF THE ENEMY

I like this one. Elisha warned the king of Israel concerning the plans of
the enemy. Elisha was hearing what the enemy king was speaking in
his bedchamber. Prophets can sometimes hear the plans of the enemy.

> The king of Israel sent word to the place of which the man of
> God spoke. He warned him and was on his guard there more
> than once.
>
> The mind of the king of Aram was troubled by this, so he
> called his servants and said to them, "Will you not tell me
> who among us sides with the king of Israel?" Then one of his
> servants said, "No one, my lord, O king. Elisha, the prophet

who is in Israel, tells the king of Israel the words that you
speak in your bedroom."

—2 KINGS 6:10–12

Prophets will see the demon others don't see. Prophets will con-
front the demon others ignore.

OASIS: REFRESHMENT AND REST

The prophetic atmosphere is an oasis (Elim). An oasis is a fertile spot
in a desert where water is found. It is a watering hole, watering place,
waterhole, spring. The prophetic refreshes, provides rest, and waters
dry places. An oasis is a place of palm trees. Elim is a picture of this.
Elim was a place of seventy palm trees in the wilderness. The prophet
is like a palm tree. If you need refreshing, get around a prophet.

Deborah, a prophetess, sat under a palm tree.

> Now Deborah, the wife of Lappidoth, was a prophetess. She
> judged Israel at that time. She would sit under the palm tree
> of Deborah between Ramah and Bethel in the hill country of
> Ephraim. The children of Israel would go up to her for her to
> render judgment.
>
> —JUDGES 4:4–5

> Then they came to Elim, where there were twelve wells of
> water and seventy palm trees, and they camped there by the
> waters.
>
> —EXODUS 15:27

Prophets help prepare us for times of refreshing.

Churches and believers need seasons of refreshing. These times of
refreshing come from the presence of the Lord.

Refresh means "to revive or reinvigorate, as with rest, food, or
drink; to renew by stimulation."

> So repent (change your mind and purpose); turn around and
> return [to God], that your sins may be erased (blotted out,
> wiped clean), that times of refreshing (of recovering from the

effects of heat, of reviving with fresh air) may come from the
presence of the Lord.

—ACTS 3:19, AMP

MIRACLES

If you want to see miracles, step out in faith on the words of a prophet.
Peter obeyed the word of the Lord and caught a great number of fish.
Prophets speak the word of the Lord and release miracles.

> Simon answered Him, "Master, we have worked all night and
> have caught nothing. But at Your word I will let down the net."
> When they had done this, they caught a great number of fish,
> and their net was tearing.
>
> —LUKE 5:5–6

Prophet's words release angels.

Angels hearken to the voice of God. When God speaks, angels
move. God speaks through His prophets.

> Praise the Lord, you powerful angels of His who do what He
> says, obeying His voice as He speaks!
>
> —PSALM 103:20, NLV

PROSPERITY

Believe God's prophets and you will prosper. Prophets want to see the
people of God prosper. Second Chronicles 20:20 says, "Believe in the
LORD your God, and you shall be established; believe His prophets,
and you shall prosper" (NKJV). This is one of my favorite verses.

Prophets hurt when they see the people struggle because of disobedience. (Consider the lamentations of Jeremiah.) God wants us to
prosper. Listening to God's voice is a key to prosperity. Prophets help
us come into prosperity.

> I alone know the plans I have for you, plans to bring you pros-
> perity and not disaster, plans to bring about the future you
> hope for.
>
> —JEREMIAH 29:11, GNT

Uzziah sought God in the days of Zechariah the prophet and prospered. Zechariah had understanding in dreams and visions. Uzziah evidently had the help of Zechariah as he sought the Lord.

> And he sought after God in the days of Zechariah, the one who instructed him in the fear of the LORD. And in the days that he sought after the LORD, God caused him to succeed.
>
> —2 CHRONICLES 26:5

LIFE

The words of a prophet give life. It is the Spirit that gives life; the flesh is useless. The Lord says, "The words that I speak to you are spirit and are life" (John 6:63). Spiritual words give life. These words contain the breath of God. Prophets speak by the Spirit, and their words are life giving. People are awakened (come alive) through prophecy and prophetic ministry.

> It is the Spirit that gives life. The body is of no value for that. But the things I have told you are from the Spirit, so they give life.
>
> —JOHN 6:63, ERV

Prophets also remind you where you have come from. Prophets tell you where you are. Prophets tell you where you are going. This is because God moves you from your past, into your present, and into your future. This is your life. God is concerned about your life (past, present, and future). Prophets can see you in all these aspects.

The prophets reminded Israel of from where God had brought them, where they were in the present, and their future.

PROPHETIC BLESSING

Prophets bless. Some people think that all prophets do is curse people, but prophets love to bless people. They love to speak words of blessing over people whom God desires to bless. Jacob blessed his sons before he died (Gen. 49). Moses blessed the tribes of Israel with prophetic words (Deut. 33).

Prophetic blessings are powerful. Your life will be changed and blessed when you are blessed by a prophet.

> This is the blessing with which Moses the man of God blessed the Israelites before his death.
>
> —Deuteronomy 33:1, amp

> Moses and Aaron went into the Tent of Meeting, and when they came out they blessed the people, and the glory of the Lord [the Shekinah cloud] appeared to all the people [as promised].
>
> —Leviticus 9:23, amp

Don't despise what prophets have to say.

> Do not spurn the gifts and utterances of the prophets [do not depreciate prophetic revelations nor despise inspired instruction or exhortation or warning].
>
> —1 Thessalonians 5:20, amp

> Don't suppress the Spirit, and don't stifle those who have a word from the Master.
>
> —1 Thessalonians 5:19–22, the message

Those who hate prophets have a long line of predecessors.

> Woe to you, scribes and Pharisees, hypocrites! You build the tombs of the prophets, and adorn the memorials of the righteous, and say, "If we lived in the days of our fathers, we would not have partaken with them in shedding the blood of the prophets." Therefore you are witnesses against yourselves that you are sons of those who murdered the prophets. Fill up, then, the measure of your fathers' guilt.
>
> —Matthew 23:29–32

A prophetic word can save your life, release you into your destiny, give you understanding, release grace into your life, bring correction, cause breakthrough, and give you direction. Prophets and prophetic utterances are sometimes despised and lightly esteemed. Prophets should be esteemed and received. They bring great blessing.

LIKE GOLD AND SILVER

The words and ministry of a prophet are valuable, and when we welcome them, they bring rewards, benefits, and blessing. Their words are like gold and silver. Prophets are vessels of gold and silver in the house of the Lord. Silver and gold are valuable. Silver and gold represent purity.

> The tongues of those who are upright and in right standing with God are as choice silver.
> —PROVERBS 10:20, AMP

> A word fitly spoken and in due season is like apples of gold in settings of silver.
> —PROVERBS 25:11, AMP

> In a large house there are not only gold and silver vessels, but also those of wood and clay; some are for honor, and some for dishonor. One who cleanses himself from these things will be a vessel for honor.
> —2 TIMOTHY 2:20–21

You are valuable, prophet. Remain clean and pure. Let nothing or no one taint you.

5

THE PROPHET'S MANIFESTO

*Jesus cried out . . . "For I have not spoken on My own
authority, but the Father who sent Me gave Me a command, what I should say and what I should speak."*

—JOHN 12:44, 49

T HE SERMON ON the Mount found in Matthew chapter 5 is the
prophet's manifesto. A manifesto is a published verbal declaration
of the intentions, motives, or views of the issuer, be it an individual, group, political party or government.

POOR IN SPIRIT

Prophets look for humility, the poor in spirit, those who recognize
their need for God.

> Blessed (happy, to be envied, and spiritually prosperous—
> with life-joy and satisfaction in God's favor and salvation,
> regardless of their outward conditions) are the poor in spirit
> (the humble, who rate themselves insignificant), for theirs is
> the kingdom of heaven!
>
> —MATTHEW 5:3, AMP

Prophets grieve (mourn) over what grieves the heart of God. They
also walk in the comfort of the Holy Ghost.

> God blesses those people who grieve. They will find comfort!
>
> —MATTHEW 5:4, CEV

MEEKNESS

Meekness is important to prophets. Meekness is characterized as
mild, patient, and long-suffering.

> Blessed (happy, blithesome, joyous, spiritually prosperous—
> with life-joy and satisfaction in God's favor and salvation,
> regardless of their outward conditions) are the meek (the
> mild, patient, long-suffering), for they shall inherit the earth!
>
> —MATTHEW 5:5, AMP

RIGHTEOUSNESS

Prophets have a hunger and thirst for righteousness (justice, uprightness, right standing with God).

> Blessed and fortunate and happy and spiritually prosperous
> (in that state in which the born-again child of God enjoys His
> favor and salvation) are those who hunger and thirst for righteousness (uprightness and right standing with God), for they
> shall be completely satisfied!
>
> —MATTHEW 5:6, AMP

MERCY

Prophets will cry out against cruelty and harshness. They call for mercy and compassion for the afflicted and oppressed.

> Blessed (happy, to be envied, and spiritually prosperous—
> with life-joy and satisfaction in God's favor and salvation,
> regardless of their outward conditions) are the merciful, for
> they shall obtain mercy!
>
> —MATTHEW 5:7, AMP

PEACEMAKING

Prophets grieve when there is strife, hatred, fighting, contention, confusion, and division. They are lovers and promoters of peace (*shalom*).

> Blessed (enjoying enviable happiness, spiritually prosperous—
> with life-joy and satisfaction in God's favor and salvation,
> regardless of their outward conditions) are the makers and
> maintainers of peace, for they shall be called the sons of God!
>
> —MATTHEW 5:9, AMP

PERSECUTED

Prophets are often persecuted for their stand for righteousness. This has always been the case. Unrighteous system will fight against anything that threatens them.

> Blessed are those who are persecuted for righteousness' sake, for theirs is the kingdom of heaven. "Blessed are you when men revile you, and persecute you, and say all kinds of evil against you falsely for My sake. Rejoice and be very glad, because great is your reward in heaven, for in this manner they persecuted the prophets who were before you."
>
> —MATTHEW 5:10–12

SALT AND LIGHT

Prophets are salt and light.

> You are the salt of the earth. But if the salt loses its saltiness, how shall it be made salty? It is from then on good for nothing but to be thrown out and to be trampled underfoot by men. You are the light of the world. A city that is set on a hill cannot be hidden. Neither do men light a candle and put it under a basket, but on a candlestick. And it gives light to all who are in the house. Let your light so shine before men that they may see your good works and glorify your Father who is in heaven.
>
> —MATTHEW 5:13–16

I know this verse is applicable to all true believers, but it is especially applicable to prophets. Prophets bring salt and light to the church and the world. Prophets cannot hide the light that God gives them. Prophets bring light to the house (the church).

UPHOLD JUSTICE

Prophets have a standard of righteousness. They teach and preach what is right. The greatest in the kingdom are the obedient. Read

Matthew 5:17–20. Jesus upheld the law because it was righteous. He fulfilled the law and the righteousness of the law. We are now righteous through Christ.

Again, the emphasis of prophets is righteousness (justice, right standing with God).

The Pharisees were not righteous. They considered themselves the greatest, but they were the least. They were actually teaching men to break the law through their tradition. The Pharisees were hypocritical.

MOTIVES OF THE HEART

Prophets warn of the consequences of unjustifiable anger (murder) and calling your brother a fool. Prophets deal with the motives of the heart. The motive in much name calling, and insult, is anger and hatred, which is murder. Read Matthew 5:21–26.

These verses are interesting as they show how Jesus (a prophet like unto Moses) views unjustifiable anger. Unjustifiable anger is when you do not have a case, but you still press it. The result of anger can be a court or a trial. The result is that it might backfire on you. Reconciliation is important before it goes that far. The results can be devastating (lawsuits), including judgment and prison. This is where unjustifiable anger can lead. Jesus likens it to murder.

Some people will make a case out of anything. This is an unrighteous use of the legal system. People use the legal system to destroy others (murder). Prophets try to help us keep our hearts clear of this level of anger.

ISSUES OF THE DAY

Prophets will deal with the issues of their day (injustice). Read Matthew 5:27–32.

Divorce was one of the issues of the day when Jesus ministered. The religious system of His day had provided a way for men to divorce their wives for almost any cause. Jesus rebuked them and exposed the real reason for these divorces—lust, adultery, and hardness of heart. The men of Christ's day were simply being cruel toward their mates in putting them away. Prophets will deal with cruelty and hardness of heart.

Malachi also dealt with this injustice and called it treachery. This was being committed by the priests in Malachi's day.

> Did He not make them one, having a remnant of the Spirit? And why one? He seeks godly offspring. So take heed to your spirit, that you do not deal treacherously. For the LORD, the God of Israel, says that He hates divorce; for it covers one's garment with violence, says the LORD of Hosts. Therefore take heed to your spirit, that you do not deal treacherously.
>
> —MALACHI 2:15–16

Again the issue was injustice. Wives were being unfairly treated by their husbands, and it was sanctioned by the religious system of the day.

> He said to them, "Moses, for the hardness of your hearts, permitted you to divorce your wives, but from the beginning it was not so.
>
> —MATTHEW 19:8

They were putting away their wives for issues other than adultery, when in fact what they were doing was a form of adultery. They were trying to use Moses's words, about issuing a bill of divorcement when they divorced their wives, as a loophole to divorce without legal grounds. Moses's decree was not an endorsement of divorce, but it was a protection for the women who were being put away, that they would have something that said they were not put away because of adultery.

Divorce is also an issue today. Divorce can be unrighteous depending on the motive. Prophets hate this and all kinds of injustice and will speak against it.

6

JONAH: PROPHETS ON THE RUN

*Now the word of the LORD came to Jonah son of Amittai,
saying, "Get up, go to Nineveh, the great city, and cry out against
it, because their wickedness has come up before Me." But Jonah
got up to flee to Tarshish from the presence of the LORD.*

—JONAH 1:1–3

THE LORD GAVE me a word in this season for all the Jonahs: Stop running from your call and assignment; you will end up in the belly of a whale. As soon as you obey, that whale will spit you out so you can complete your assignment.

Where shall I go from Your spirit, or where shall I flee from Your presence? If I ascend to heaven, You are there; if I make my bed in Sheol, You are there. If I take the wings of the morning and dwell at the end of the sea, even there Your hand shall guide me, and Your right hand shall take hold of me.

If I say, "Surely the darkness shall cover me, and the light shall be as night about me," even the darkness is not dark to You, but the night shines as the day, for the darkness is like light to You.

—PSALM 139:7–12

ARE YOU A JONAH?

Are you a prophet on the run? Are you running away from your assignment to speak the word of the Lord? Are you running from the presence of the Lord? Are you hiding? You can run, but you cannot hide from God.

The Lord is calling the Jonahs. You will not be the first, and you will not be the last. There are Jonahs in every generation. There are prophets running from God today. Don't be a prophet on the run. You have been called to bless your generation. Don't run and hide from the call. Embrace it and obey God today.

For those who don't want to speak for the Lord, I pray that His word in your heart will be like fire shut up in your bones (Jer. 20:9)!

God told Jonah to arise and go to Nineveh. Jonah instead went the other way. Jonah ran from the presence of the Lord. There are many prophets who are like Jonah. I call them prophets on the run. They sense and know the call of God to be a prophet, but they say, "I cannot handle that calling."

If you are a prophet on the run, then you know that you cannot hide from God. You cannot hide in the bottom of the ship as Jonah did. You cannot hide from the presence of the Lord.

In Psalm 139:8–9, 12 David wrote, "If I ascend to heaven, You are there; if I make my bed in Sheol, You are there. If I take the wings of the morning and dwell at the end of the sea…, even the darkness is not dark to You, but the night shines as the day, for the darkness is like light to You." Even the darkness cannot hide from God. Jonah tried to hide, but God knew where he was. God knows where His Jonahs are. He knows where every prophet is.

ARISE AND GO TO NINEVEH!

Jonah did go to Nineveh. Jonah did speak the word of the Lord to that city. The results were astonishing. The whole city repented and was spared.

Jonah's assignment was to speak to a city. What is your assignment? How many lives hang in the balance as a result of your calling? How many people will be blessed when you obey God?

This is a call for the Jonahs to arise and go to Nineveh. Where is your Nineveh? Whom are you sent to? These are questions every prophet has to answer.

YOUR JONAH EXPERIENCE HAS PROPHETIC SIGNIFICANCE

Even Jonah's experience was prophetic. He was in the belly of the whale three days and three nights. This was a picture of Christ being in the heart of the earth three days and three nights.

> For as Jonah was three days and three nights in the belly of the great fish, so will the Son of Man be three days and three nights in the heart of the earth.
> —MATTHEW 12:40

When you are prophetic even your experiences will be prophetic. Jonah was prophetic even when he was running away from the call. Prophet, you can't escape. You have been designed by God to be a prophet. You will see things even when you are running from the call.

> Then they said to Jonah, "What shall we do to you, so that the sea may quiet down for us?" For the sea was growing stormier So Jonah said to them, "Pick me up and toss me into the sea. Then the sea will quiet down for you. For I know that it is on my account this great storm has come upon you."
> —JONAH 1:11–12

Jonah knew what was going on when the storm came. The men on the ship did not know, but Jonah knew. Prophets know when they are running. They know the trouble of running from the call. Jonah told the men to throw him overboard. Then he was swallowed by a big fish. Jonah cried out to God from the belly of the big fish. He promised God he would pay his vows.

Prophets, many of you have vowed to serve and obey the Lord, but you are running the other way. It is time to keep your vows, promises, dedications, and obligations.

> But I will sacrifice to You with the voice of thanksgiving; I will pay what I have vowed. Salvation is of the LORD!
> —JONAH 2:9

> Your vows are on me, O God; I will complete them with thank offerings to You.
>
> —Psalm 56:12

The story of Jonah shows us the importance of the call of the prophet. Prophets are different. Prophets are unique. Prophets don't ask to be called or chosen. Prophets are called from the womb. Prophets pay a price for running and hiding. Jonah ended up in the belly of a great fish.

Necessity Is Laid Upon You

> For though I preach the gospel, I have nothing to glory of: for necessity is laid upon me; yea, woe is unto me, if I preach not the gospel!
>
> —1 Corinthians 9:16, kjv

Arise and obey, Jonah. Don't get yourself in trouble. Necessity is laid upon you. You have to obey God. You have to arise. Jonah prayed, and God brought him out of the fish's belly. God will bring you forth when you pray.

There are many ministers who have accepted the call to preach but are running from the prophetic calling. Maybe your group does not believe in prophets. Maybe you have seen people call themselves prophets who did not have good character. Maybe you have seen false prophets. These are reasons why some run from the call.

God is calling and transitioning many of His ministers. Many have been called to be prophets, but they are fearful. Don't be a Jonah. Don't run from the call. Embrace it. The prophet's ministry is designed to bring deliverance and salvation to many. Nineveh was spared and blessed because Jonah went there.

No Excuses for Prophets

The call to be a prophet can seem intimidating. The prophet's call is a great responsibility. Some prophets come up with excuses, but God does not want to hear them.

Jeremiah said, "I am too young." Moses said, "I am not eloquent." God answered them both.

> And the LORD said to [Moses], "Who has made man's mouth? Or who made the dumb, or deaf, or the seeing, or the blind? Have not I, the LORD?"
>
> —EXODUS 4:11

> But the LORD said to me, "Do not say, 'I am a youth.' For you shall go everywhere that I send you, and whatever I command you, you shall speak."
>
> —JEREMIAH 1:7

God will make a way for you too and will back you up when He calls you. God's grace is sufficient. Don't be afraid. You can do this.

APPEAL TO THE JONAHS

If you have been running, then you need to repent and turn around. Don't waste another day not doing what God has called you to do. Make a decision today. Obey God. Don't obey your flesh. Don't submit to your fears. Don't be rebellious. Repent before it is too late. Repent like Jonah. Jonah cried unto the Lord, and God heard him. It is better to say no, and then turn around, than to say yes and never do it. Notice the parable of Jesus in Matthew's Gospel:

> What do you think? A man had two sons. He came to the first and said, "Son, go work today in my vineyard." He answered, "I will not," but afterward he repented and went. Then he came to the second, and said likewise. He answered, "I will go, sir," but did not go. Which of the two did the will of his father? They said, "The first." Jesus said to them, "Truly I say to you, the tax collectors and prostitutes enter the kingdom of God before you."
>
> —MATTHEW 21:28–31

The son who said, "I will not," but later repented and went into the vineyard, did the will of his father. Repent and do the will of the Father. Go into the vineyard and work.

PRAYERS OF REPENTANCE FOR JONAHS

Lord, I repent for running from my calling.

I will turn around and obey the call.

I will not be rebellious anymore.

I will not allow fear or rebellion to cause me to run from the prophet's call.

I submit my life to You, Lord.

I submit my tongue to speak Your word.

I submit my eyes to see Your vision.

I submit my life and time to being a prophetic voice.

I accept my assignment and the grace I need to fulfill it.

I will not be a Jonah.

I will go to my Nineveh.

I will speak Your word.

Let any trouble I have experienced in running from the call leave my life.

Let Your peace return to my life.

Let Your joy return to my life.

I renounce and turn away from any behavior that is contrary to the prophet's call.

I turn away from any religious tradition that would keep me from obeying this call.

I will not be afraid to do what I have been sent to do.

7

HEALING AND DELIVERANCE
FOR THE PROPHET

*Then your light shall break forth as the morning, and your
healing shall spring forth quickly, and your righteousness shall
go before you; the glory of the LORD shall be your reward.*

—ISAIAH 58:8

MANY PROPHETS ARE in need of healing and restoration. Prophets are very sensitive and must guard their hearts. Prophets can take rejection personally. Prophets can experience deep hurt and pain. Even Elijah, one of Israel's greatest prophets, felt alone and isolated.

> And he said, "I have been very jealous for the LORD, Lord of Hosts, for the children of Israel have forsaken Your covenant, thrown down Your altars, and killed Your prophets with the sword, and I alone am left, and they seek to take my life."
>
> —1 KINGS 19:10

Elijah was also tired after his encounter with the false prophets of Jezebel on Mount Carmel. Tired prophets need God's strength. Prophets can expend a lot of virtue in their functions. Prophets sometimes overextend themselves. Jesus said, "Come away...and rest" (Mark 6:31). There are times prophets need to be refreshed and strengthened from heaven.

Don't be discouraged, prophet. You can become tired like everyone else. God will refresh and restore you.

> The angel of the LORD came again a second time and touched him and said, "Arise and eat, because the journey is too great for you." He arose and ate and drank and went in the strength

of that food forty days and forty nights to Horeb, the mountain of God.

—1 Kings 19:7–8

Loose the Bands of Your Neck

Satan hates prophets and will do anything to destroy them. The prophet is a threat to the works of darkness. The prophet is a target to the powers of hell. Prophets can also slip into pride and become too harsh and critical.

But you can arise from the dust. Shake yourself. Loose the bands of your neck. You will not be held captive by Satan or by men. You will not be held captive by religious tradition.

> Shake thyself from the dust; arise, and sit down, O Jerusalem: loose thyself from the bands of thy neck, O captive daughter of Zion.
>
> —Isaiah 52:2, kjv

There is deliverance and restoration for prophets. There is healing from rejection and hurt. There is deliverance from fear and apprehension.

There is deliverance from the assignment of the spirit of Jezebel. The spirit of Jezebel hates prophets and attempts to wipe them out. In the Bible Jezebel was a witch. Her idolatry and witchcrafts were many.

Demons That Attack Prophets

Other spirits that attack prophets include:

- Rejection (self-rejection, fear of rejection)
- Witchcraft
- Fear
- Loneliness
- Intimidation
- Isolation
- Discouragement
- Anger
- Hurt
- Insecurity

+ Depression
+ Frustration
+ Weariness
+ Pride
+ Confusion
+ Jealousy (against prophets)
+ Burnout
+ Tiredness
+ Bitterness
+ Unforgiveness

+ Inferiority
+ Disappointment
+ Timidity
+ Shyness
+ Lust
+ Deception (self-deception)
+ Withdrawal
+ Grief
+ Sadness
+ Infirmity

Loose yourself from these spirits. You may not be attacked by them all, but the ones that have affected you need to be dealt with.

MY PRAYER FOR HEALING AND DELIVERANCE TO COME TO PROPHETS

Agree with me on this prayer for you and other prophets among us. You can also rework this prayer as you are led and pray it directly over yourself to see yourself set free to accomplish the call of God on your life.

I pray right now, in the name of Jesus, that every curse spoken against prophets be annulled. Let every negative word spoken against you be canceled. Let every attack of witchcraft, including intimidation, be canceled.

I command these spirits to loose the prophets and let them go. I command them to come out in the name of Jesus. I command you to be healed and restored in your emotions. I command every attack on your mind to be canceled.

I command all spirits of fear to go. Anything that would intimidate you and make you afraid to speak the word of the Lord must go, in the name of Jesus. Fear of rejection, go. Fear of man, go. Fear of being misunderstood, go. Fear of being persecuted, go.

All spirits attacking your mind must leave in the name of Jesus. All spirits that make you think you are crazy, go. Spirits that want to control the way you think, go.

All spirits attacking your body, leave in the name of Jesus. All spirits of sickness and infirmity, go.

I pray for your emotions to be healed. I command all rejection to leave in the name of Jesus. I command all hurt and deep hurt to go. I command your heart to be healed and to be made whole. I command your soul to be restored.

Any prophet with a wounded spirit or broken heart, be healed. I pray that God would mend your heart and comfort you. I pray that all your wounds be bound up. Let the oil and wine of healing be poured into your life.

I command all spirits that make you feel inferior or unworthy to come out. All spirits of guilt, shame, and condemnation go in the name of Jesus.

I command all spirits of double-mindedness to leave in the name of Jesus. All spirits that make you waver and be inconsistent, come out in the name of Jesus.

I command all spirits of wrath and anger to go. All spirits of unforgiveness and bitterness due to hurt and rejection, go.

I command all spirits of pride to leave in the name of Jesus. All spirits of arrogance and haughtiness, go. All spirits of ego and vanity, leave.

I command all spirits of isolation and loneliness to come out in the name of Jesus. All spirits of depression and discouragement, go. Any spirit that makes you want to give up and quit, leave now.

I command any spirit that would attack you at night to leave. All spirits of insomnia and restlessness, go.

I pray that you would be healed from hurt from pastors, churches, networks, family, and friends. I pray that you would be healed from any betrayal and treachery. I pray that you would be delivered from false friends and false brethren.

I command all spirits of disappointment to leave in the name of Jesus. Disappointment with pastors, churches, and the saints, go in the name of Jesus.

I pray that your joy would be restored and be full.

I pray for the zeal of God to be restored to you.

I pray that a fresh anointing to prophesy will fall upon you.

I pray that you will have a fresh anointing to dream and have visions.

I pray that anything blocking or hindering your prophetic flow be removed in the name of Jesus. Let any dam that is blocking the flow of the Holy Spirit be removed.

I pray for your ears to be opened. I pray for anything stopping or blocking you from hearing the voice of God to be removed. Let your ears be unplugged. Let your ears and mind be unstopped.

Let the rivers of living water flow out of your belly. Let the prophetic bubble up and gush from you. Let the word of the Lord drop from heaven on you. Let the word fall like rain upon your life.

I pray that you would be filled with the Holy Ghost. I pray that your cup will overflow. I pray that you would be filled with Holy Ghost boldness.

I pray that you would be filled with the wisdom of God. You will have the wisdom of God to fulfill your assignment.

8

PRAYERS AND DECLARATIONS TO RELEASE THE PROPHET IN YOU

Call to Me, and I will answer you, and show you great and mighty things which you do not know.

—JEREMIAH 33:3

Lord, give me strength to bring forth my destiny as Your prophet (Isa. 66:9).

Lord, let me not operate in the wrong spirit (Luke 9:55).

Let me have and walk in an excellent spirit (Dan. 6:3).

Lord, stir up my spirit to do Your will (Hag. 1:14).

I reject all false prophetic ministry in the name of Jesus (2 Pet. 2:1).

I reject the mouth of vanity and the right hand of falsehood (Ps. 144:8).

I reject every false vision and every false prophetic word released into my life (Jer. 14:14).

I bind Satan, the deceiver, from releasing any deception into my life (Rev. 12:9).

I bind and cast out all spirits of self-deception in the name of Jesus (1 Cor. 3:18).

I bind and cast out any spirit of sorcery that would deceive me in the name of Jesus (Rev. 18:23).

Lord, let no man deceive me (Matt. 24:4).

I bind and rebuke any bewitchment that would keep me from obeying the truth (Gal. 3:1).

I pray for utterance and boldness to make known the mystery of the gospel (Eph. 6:19).

I bind and cast out any spirit of Absalom that would try to steal my heart from God's ordained leadership (2 Sam. 15:6).

Lord, cleanse my life from secret faults (Ps. 19:12).

Lord, let Your secret be upon my tabernacle (Job 29:4).

Lead me and guide me for Your name's sake (Ps. 31:3).

Guide me continually (Isa. 58:11).

Guide me into all truth (John 16:13).

Guide me with Your eye (Ps. 32:8).

Let me guide my affairs with discretion (Ps. 112:5).

Guide me by the skillfulness of Your hands (Ps. 78:72).

Lead me in a plain path because of my enemies (Ps. 27:11).

Lead me not into temptation, but deliver me from evil (Matt. 6:13).

Lead me, and make Your way straight before my eyes (Ps. 5:8).

Make the crooked places straight and the rough places smooth before me (Isa. 40:4).

Send out Your light and truth, and let them lead me (Ps. 43:3).

Make darkness light before me and crooked things straight (Isa. 42:16).

Lord, give me wisdom in every area where I lack (James 1:5).

PRAYERS THAT RELEASE PROPHETIC REVELATION

You are a God that reveals secrets. Lord, reveal Your secrets unto me (Dan. 2:28).

Reveal to me the secret and deep things (Dan. 2:22).

Let me understand things kept secret from the foundation of the world (Matt. 13:35).

Let the seals be broken from Your Word (Dan. 12:9).

Let me understand and have revelation of Your will and purpose.

Give me the spirit of wisdom and revelation, and let the eyes of my understanding be enlightened (Eph. 1:17).

Let me understand heavenly things (John 3:12).

Open my eyes to behold wondrous things out of Your Word (Ps. 119:18)

Let me know and understand the mysteries of the kingdom (Mark 4:11).

Let me speak to others by revelation (1 Cor. 14:6).

Reveal Your secrets to Your servants the prophets (Amos 3:7).

Let the hidden things be made manifest (Mark 4:22).

Hide Your truths from the wise and prudent, and reveal them to babes (Matt. 11:25).

Let Your arm be revealed in my life (John 12:38).

Reveal the things that belong to me (Deut. 29:29).

Let Your Word be revealed unto me (1 Sam. 3:7).

Let Your glory be revealed in my life (Isa. 40:5).

Let Your righteousness be revealed in my life (Isa. 56:1).

Let me receive visions and revelations of the Lord (2 Cor. 12:1).

Let me receive an abundance of revelations (2 Cor. 12:7).

Let me be a good steward of Your revelations (1 Cor. 4:1).

Let me speak the mystery of Christ (Col. 4:3).

Let me receive and understand Your hidden wisdom (1 Cor. 2:7).

Hide not Your commandments from me (Ps. 119:19).

Let me speak the wisdom of God in a mystery (1 Cor. 2:7).

Let me make known the mystery of the gospel (Eph. 6:19).

Make known unto me the mystery of Your will (Eph. 1:9).

Open Your dark sayings upon the harp (Ps. 49:4).

Let me understand Your parables; the words of the wise and their dark sayings (Prov. 1:6).

Lord, light my candle and enlighten my darkness (Ps. 18:28).

Make darkness light before me (Isa. 42:16).

Give me the treasures of darkness and hidden riches in secret places (Isa. 45:3).

Let Your candle shine upon my head (Job 29:3).

My spirit is the candle of the Lord, searching all the inward parts of the belly (Prov. 20:27).

Let me understand the deep things of God (1 Cor. 2:10).

Let me understand Your deep thoughts (Ps. 92:5).

Let my eyes be enlightened with Your Word (Ps. 19:8).

My eyes are blessed to see (Luke 10:23).

Let all spiritual cataracts and scales be removed from my eyes (Acts 9:18).

Let me comprehend with all saints what is the breadth and length and depth and height of Your love (Eph. 3:18).

Let my reins instruct me in the night season, and let me awaken with revelation (Ps. 16:7).

Prayers That Break the Power of Jezebel

I loose the hounds of heaven against Jezebel (1 Kings 21:23).

I rebuke and bind the spirits of witchcraft, lust, seduction, intimidation, idolatry, and whoredom connected to Jezebel.

I release the spirit of Jehu against Jezebel and her cohorts (2 Kings 9:30–33).

I command Jezebel to be thrown down and eaten by the hounds of heaven.

I rebuke all spirits of false teaching, false prophecy, idolatry, and perversion connected with Jezebel (Rev. 2:20).

I loose tribulation against the kingdom of Jezebel (Rev. 2:22).

I cut off the assignment of Jezebel against the ministers of God (1 Kings 19:2).

I cut off and break the powers of every word released by Jezebel against my life.

I cut off Jezebel's table and reject all food from it (1 Kings 18:19).

I cut off and loose myself from all curses of Jezebel and spirits of Jezebel operating in my bloodline.

I cut off the assignment of Jezebel and her daughters to corrupt the church.

I rebuke and cut off the spirit of Athaliah that attempts to destroy the royal seed (2 Kings 11:1).

I come against the spirit of Herodias and cut off the assignment to kill the prophets (Mark 6:22–24).

I rebuke and cut off the spirit of whoredoms (Hosea 4:12).

I rebuke and cut off Jezebel and her witchcrafts in the name of Jesus (2 Kings 9:22).

I rebuke and cut off the harlot and mistress of witchcrafts and break her power over my life and family (Nah. 3:4).

I cut off witchcrafts out of the hands (Mic. 5:12).

I overcome Jezebel and receive power over the nations (Rev. 2:26).

PRAYERS TO RELEASE THE PROPHETS IN YOUR FAMILY

Lord, pour out Your Spirit upon my family, and let the sons and daughters prophesy.

Lord, put Your words in the mouth of my seed and my seed's seed.

Let my family members speak Your words with confidence and boldness.

Let the spirit of prophecy be released upon my family members, in the name of Jesus.

Let my family members have dreams and visions by the Spirit of the Lord.

Let the gifts of the Holy Spirit be released in abundance to the members of my family.

Let my family be set in the church and be used by You to minister prophetically.

The word of the Lord has been spoken to all who are in my family (Acts 16:32).

Let the word of the Lord come to my family (Ps. 107:20).

The word of the Lord will be spread out among my family (Acts 13:49).

My family will be numbered according to the word of the Lord (Num. 3:16).

My family will hear the word of the Lord (2 Kings 20:16).

The word of the Lord over my family is right, and all His work is done in truth (Ps. 33:4).

The word of the Lord grows mightily in my family and will prevail (Acts 19:20).

The Lord will reveal Himself to my family by the word of the Lord (1 Sam. 3:21).

The word of the Lord is proven in my family. It is a shield to all of us who trust in Him (2 Sam. 22:31).

My family will go and do according to the word of the Lord (1 Kings 17:5).

My family will inquire for the word of the Lord today (1 Kings 22:5).

The word of the Lord tests my family (Ps. 105:19).

The word of the Lord comes to my family now (Jer. 17:15).

By the word of the Lord that endures forever, the gospel will be preached to my family (1 Pet. 1:25).

All the words that the Lord has said, my family will do (Exod. 24:3).

The word of the Lord comes to my family and says, "Do not be afraid....I am your shield, your exceedingly great reward" (Gen. 15:1, NKJV).

Let the word of the Lord be common among my family. Let there be widespread revelation (1 Sam. 3:1).

The word of the Lord in the mouths of my loved ones is the truth (1 Kings 17:24).

The word of the Lord is with my family (2 Kings 3:12).

The words of the Lord over my family are pure words, like silver tried in a furnace, purified seven times (Ps. 12:6).

Let my family receive the word of the Lord so that we may have wisdom (Jer. 8:9).

The word of the Lord runs swiftly in my family and is glorified (2 Thess. 3:1).

My family shall give heed to the word of the Lord (Jer. 6:10).

The women in my family will hear the word of the Lord and will receive the word of His mouth (Jer. 9:20).

The word of the Lord is with my family, and we make intercession to the Lord of hosts (Jer. 27:18).

My family shall hear the word of the Lord: "You will not die by the sword" (Jer. 34:4).

My family will not suffer a famine of hearing the words of the Lord, in Jesus's name (Amos 8:11).

My family will go to the land of our possession, which we have obtained according to the word of the Lord (Josh. 22:9).

NOTES

CHAPTER 1
THE MAKING OF A PROPHET

1. Leonard Ravenhill, "The Picture of a Prophet," Ravenhill.org, http://www.ravenhill.org/prophet.htm (accessed April 28, 2015).

2. Jake Kail, "Balaam and Jezebel: Two Types of False Prophets," JakeKail.com, October 7, 2013, http://www.jakekail.com/balaam-jezebel-types-false-prophets/ (accessed April 28, 2015).

3. Art Katz, "The Prophetic Function," AuthenticTheology.com, http://www.authentictheology.com/blog/terms-concepts/the-prophetic-function-by-art-katz/ (accessed April 28, 2015).

4. Theresa Harvard Johnson, "Scribal Prophets, Apostles and Scribal Ministry," Prophetic-Writing-School.com, http://prophetic-writing-school.com/8-scribal-prophets/3-what-is-a-scribal-prophet (accessed April 28, 2015).

5. Joseph Mattera, "The Difference Between Apostolic and Prophetic Roles," Charismamag.com, January 23, 2013, http://www.charismamag.com/spirit/prophecy/16593-how-do-you-know-the-difference-between-apostolic-and-prophetic-functions (accessed April 28, 2015).

6. Oxforddictionaries.com, s.v. "synergy," http://www.oxforddictionaries.com/us/definition/american_english/synergy (accessed April 28, 2015).

7. Michael Sullivant, "How to Stay Humble in Prophetic Ministry," CharismaMag.com, http://www.charismamag.com/life/1370-j15/slw-spiritual-growth-/prophecy/9594-humility-in-the-prophetic-ministry (accessed April 28, 2015).

8. Patricia Bootsma, "The Hidden Life of the Prophetic Voice," Revival Mag.com, May 7, 2013, http://revivalmag.com/article/hidden-life-prophetic-voice (accessed April 28, 2015).

9. "John Emerich Edward Dalberg Acton, 1st Baron Acton Quotes," Britannica.com, http://www.britannica.com/EBchecked/topic/4647/

John-Emerich-Edward-Dalberg-Acton-1st-Baron-Acton (accessed April 28, 2015).

10. R. C. Sproul Jr., "Ask RC: Why Did the Pharisees Hate Jesus So Much?" RCSproulJr.com, http://rcsprouljr.com/blog/ask-rc/rc-pharisees-hate-jesus-much/ (accessed April 28, 2015).

11. Art Katz, "The Prophetic Function," AuthenticTheology.com, http://www.authentictheology.com/blog/terms-concepts/the-prophetic-function-by-art-katz/ (accessed April 28, 2015).

12. Ron McKenzie, "Role of the Prophet," KingWatch.co.nz, http://kingwatch.co.nz/Prophetic_Ministry/role.htm (accessed April 28, 2015).

13. Helen Calder, "Prophetic Intercession, Its Power and Its Pitfalls," EnlivenPublishing.com, August 6, 2012, http://www.enlivenpublishing.com/blog/tag/prophetic-intercessor/ (accessed April 28, 2015).

14. B. Dale, "A Company of Prophets," Biblehub.com, http://biblehub.com/sermons/auth/dale/a_company_of_prophets.htm (accessed April 28, 2014).

15. Ashish Raichur, *Understanding the Prophetic* (n.p., All Peoples Church, 2010), 202.

16. "School of the Prophets in the Bible," The Well Prophetic Institute, http://www.thewellchurch.net/ministries/training-and-equipping/prophetic-institute/ (accessed April 28, 2015).

17. Don A. Hoglund, "The History of Americans Towns—Prophetstown, Illinois," DonHoglund.Hubpages.com, http://dahoglund.hubpages.com/hub/History-of-American-Towns-Part-IX-Prophetstown-Illinois (accessed April 28, 2015).

CHAPTER 2
CHARACTERISTICS OF A PROPHET

1. Dennis Bratcher, "Prophets Today?" Christian Resource Institute, http://www.crivoice.org/prophetstoday.html (accessed April 28, 2015).

2. Sandy Warner, *Discernment: Separating the Holy From the Profane* (N.p.: SOS Publications, 2014).

CHAPTER 3
WHAT MOVES THE HEART OF A PROPHET?

1. David K. Blomgren, *The Song of the Lord* (Porland, OR: Bible Press, 1978), as quoted on David K. Blomgren, "The Power of Anointed Worship Music," Secret Place Ministries, http://www.secretplace ministries.org/pages/journey/soaking/anointed-worship-music.html (accessed April 28, 2015).

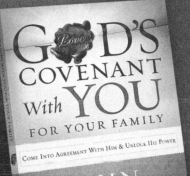